TAINTED BLOOD

Tom Jacobson

BROADWAY PLAY PUBLISHING INC
224 E 62nd St, NY, NY 10065
www.broadwayplaypub.com
info@broadwayplaypub.com

TAINTED BLOOD
© Copyright 2010 by Tom Jacobson

First printing: June 2010
I S B N: 978-0-88145-433-8

Book design: Marie Donovan
Typographic controls: Adobe InDesign
Typeface: Palatino
Printed and bound in the U S A

CHARACTERS

OSCAR WILDE, *twenty-four, an attractive professor of aesthetics*

TY, *eighteen, an angelic cockney groom*

PROFESSOR DVAPARA, *twenty-nine, a handsome Indian mesmerist*

FLORENCE BALCOMBE, *twenty, Oscar's beautiful fiancée*

OCTAVIA BALCOMBE, *fifty-five,* FLORENCE's *stolid aunt*

MISS CAMILLA QUIMBY, *twenty-two, Oscar's lusty housemaid*

BRAM STOKER, *thirty-one, a tall, red-headed acting manager*

ARTHUR CONAN DOYLE, *nineteen, an intellectual medical student*

SETTING

The action takes place in the Victorian drawing room of Moytura, the Wilde family country home on the shore of Lough Corrib in Ireland. It is late September, 1878.

Upstage double panelled doors lead to a hallway. Downstage two sets of French doors face each other from opposite sides of the stage. The French doors are framed by heavy velvet drapes with gauzy draperies beneath. The rest of the room is dark and Victorian, lit by gas lamps. The furniture includes a bookcase, a large cupboard or wardrobe, and a couch or settee. For the Prologue, the graveyard may be represented through lighting and a headstone or two.

PROLOGUE
A graveyard

ACT ONE
A drawing room
The wee hours of the morning

ACT TWO
The same
The next evening

ACT THREE
The same
Later that night

PROLOGUE
(optional)

(*A single gas streetlamp dimly illuminates a run-down
Gaelic graveyard late at night. A well-dressed* GENTLEMAN
*comes warily into the cemetery, looking anxiously for
someone. Seeing no one, he settles down to wait, fidgeting
nervously. Looking down at the ground he notices something
lying there, watches it a moment, then picks it up. It is a
worm. He takes a handkerchief from his pocket and puts the
worm in it. He searches the ground until he finds another
worm and adds it to his collection. He continues finding
worms and does not notice an angelic* BOY *come into the
cemetery. Dressed in dirty work clothes, the* BOY *is also
nervous, glancing about furtively until he sees the* MAN.
The BOY *relaxes; amused by the* MAN's *worm-gathering,
he assumes an air of smug nonchalance and stares at the*
MAN. *Finally the* MAN *notices the* BOY *and freezes. He puts
the handkerchief of worms in his pocket and stands. He and
the* BOY *stare at each other, challenging each other to make
the first move. Behind the* BOY *a* FIGURE *appears, barely
distinguishable among the shadows. The* MAN *starts to take
a step toward the* BOY *then freezes again when he sees the*
FIGURE. *The* BOY, *puzzled, turns to follow the* MAN's *gaze,
sees the* FIGURE *and starts to bolt. But he stops and turns
back to the* FIGURE, *staring at it as if hypnotized. He takes a
few slow steps toward the* FIGURE, *hesitates, then approaches
the* FIGURE *in awe. The* BOY *reaches out and touches the*
FIGURE's *voluminous dark cape, stroking the luxurious*

fabric with a combination of veneration and desire. The FIGURE *does not move. The* BOY *turns back for a moment and looks almost dismissively at the* MAN, *then disappears behind a tall headstone with the* FIGURE. *The* MAN *runs away. From behind the tombstone comes a sharp cry of pain mingled with ecstasy.)*

ACT ONE

(FLORENCE BALCOMBE, *twenty, a beautiful dark-haired woman, reclines languidly on a couch or settee in an oppressively Victorian drawing room. Across the room her rather monumental aunt,* OCTAVIA BALCOMBE, *fifty-five, sits rigidly in an overstuffed chair, reading a thick book.* OCTAVIA*'s most distinguishing feature is her enormous mound of bouffant hair. They do not speak.* FLORENCE *is almost asleep;* OCTAVIA *is stonily silent. Into this silence through the hall doors bursts a golden-haired maid,* MISS CAMILLA QUIMBY, *a lusty, lively wench. She carries an elegant plate of sandwiches and offers one to* OCTAVIA.)

MISS QUIMBY: (*Cockney*) Sandwich, mum?

OCTAVIA: (*Stentorian*) Cucumber?

MISS QUIMBY: Watercress, mum.

(OCTAVIA *rudely returns to her book.*)

OCTAVIA: Kept awake all hours with no cucumber sandwiches. Your Mister Wilde is most thoughtless, most thoughtless indeed. Ireland in September! Pfff!

(MISS QUIMBY *offers a sandwich to* FLORENCE, *who politely refuses.*)

FLORENCE: (*Tired, but gracious*) But, Aunt, green is your favorite color. You adore it.

(MISS QUIMBY *takes the plate to a corner and eats a sandwich with relish.*)

OCTAVIA: The only green item I can abide is a cucumber sandwich and there are none present. Kindly ask your mother to chaperone your next excursion to this wretched island.

FLORENCE: Aunt, I miss London as well. But Oscar's been terribly moody since he graduated, so I beg you—

(OSCAR WILDE, *twenty-four, rushes in through the hall door. He is dressed quite elegantly, is dark-haired and interesting-looking, and speaks and gestures passionately with quick humor.*)

OSCAR: Dreadfully sorry! No answer at the rectory, so we must assume our Professor Dvapara is either on his way or has been devoured by the legendary monster of the Lough. (*He goes to* OCTAVIA.) Mrs Balcombe, has Miss Quimby made you comfortable for our grand diversion?

OCTAVIA: My dear Mister Wilde, it is not possible for human persons to be comfortable at this forsaken hour in anything other than a recumbent posture. If your conjurer does not arrive within the half hour, I must insist you release me to my room.

OSCAR: Absolutely, Mrs Balcombe. (*He goes to* FLORENCE *and kneels, taking her hand.*) My darling, don't go to sleep yet. Where are Bram and Arthur?

FLORENCE: They've gone in search of you.

OSCAR: Not far, I hope. Professor Dvapara will be here soon and we'll have a delightful evening.

FLORENCE: (*Smiling tiredly*) Oscar, we're about to have a delightful morning.

OSCAR: (*Taking out his handkerchief*) I've brought you a gift to stimulate you to wakefulness. Death itself!

(OSCAR *dangles a worm in front of* FLORENCE.)

FLORENCE: (*Leaping up*) Oh, Oscar! Take it away! A worm!

OCTAVIA: Disgusting! Pfff!

FLORENCE: It's wriggling most unpleasantly!

OCTAVIA: Bordering on undulation!

OSCAR: (*Laughing*) Florence, darling, worms don't bite. While we live.

FLORENCE: Nonetheless it's slimy and a lurid color.

OSCAR: It's pink.

FLORENCE: The color of flesh.

OSCAR: (*Musing*) I did find it in the churchyard.

OCTAVIA: Pray don't make light of mortality, Mister Wilde.

OSCAR: Certainly not. It's the one thing that makes life bearable.

FLORENCE: Oscar, you've developed a most unhealthy preoccupation with death.

OSCAR: (*Placing the worm back in the handkerchief*) No, my dear. I'm preoccupied with symbolism.

OCTAVIA: (*Rising grandly*) Mister Wilde, I shall now retire. Should I dream of larvae, I blame your unusual amusements.

OSCAR: No, no, stay! The mesmerist will arrive shortly, I promise!

FLORENCE: Promise?

OSCAR: (*Leaves the worms on the bookcase, goes to* FLORENCE.) Lady, by yonder glorious moon I swear, that tips with silver all these orchard boughs—

FLORENCE: (*Turns to him, smiling as she accuses him.*) Paraphrase! A fine aesthetician you are!

(FLORENCE *and* OSCAR *start to kiss, then notice* OCTAVIA *staring at them, and stop.*)

OSCAR: (*To* OCTAVIA) Madame, I beg your forbearance.

OCTAVIA: Pfff!

(*When* OCTAVIA *turns away,* OSCAR *tries to steal a kiss from* FLORENCE, *but* BRAM STOKER *hurries into the room.* BRAM, *thirty, is a tall red-headed and red-bearded fellow, very down-to-earth. Following him is a slim medical student,* ARTHUR CONAN DOYLE, *nineteen, who is carrying a stone sivalinga.*)

BRAM: Wilde, haven't missed it all, have we?

OSCAR: Not at all. Professor Dvapara appears to have disappeared. Arthur, what are you doing with my sivalinga?

BRAM: He noticed it in the hallway and became obsessed with it.

OSCAR: Look, Florence—another symbol.

FLORENCE: Symbols, symbols, symbols! Give me something actual!

ARTHUR: Third century A D, isn't it?

OCTAVIA: What does it symbolize, Mister Wilde?

(*Embarrassed pause. The linga, although stubby, is distinctly phallic.*)

OSCAR: Fertility, dear lady. The Hindoos anoint it with milk and clarified butter as a form of worship.

ARTHUR: If this mesmerist's an Indian, perhaps he'll demonstrate for us.

BRAM: We don't need some darky to show us. Wilde's a published expert in ancient mumbo-jumbo.

FLORENCE: Mister Stoker, don't be a sycophant.

OSCAR: As Florence frequently reminds me, I'm just a plagiarist.

OSCAR & FLORENCE: But a brilliant one. (*They laugh.*)

BRAM: But the Newdigate poetry prize—

OSCAR: (*Interrupting* BRAM, *as he picks up a piece of furniture.*) Help me arrange this for the mesmerist, my good fellow?

(BRAM *helps* OSCAR *rearrange the furniture.*)

MISS QUIMBY: (*To* ARTHUR, *seductively*) Sandwich, sir?

ARTHUR: (*Bewitched, he puts down the linga.*) Why no, I mean, yes, thanks very—much, yes.

BRAM: (*Taking a small Buddha from his pocket.*) Do you suppose he'll appraise this for me?

(MISS QUIMBY *continues vamping* ARTHUR.)

OSCAR: A terra-cotta Buddha? Has Orientalism been demoted to fashion? I must find a new diversion.

BRAM: It was a gift.

OSCAR: I suppose you chant as well?

BRAM: (*Irritated, he puts the Buddha back in his pocket.*) He probably won't come anyway. It's far too late.

FLORENCE: My sentiments precisely, Mister Stoker.

OSCAR: It's the only time I could get him. Such fellows are much in demand these days.

(BRAM *takes out a note and tries to surreptitiously hand it to* FLORENCE, *but she ignores him.*)

ARTHUR: (*His mouth full.*) Charlatans will always be popular—with the ill-educated. What nonsense! Otherworld communications, tipping tables and the like.

BRAM: (*Sotto voce to* OSCAR) Wish I had a fiancee to compare with Florence. How's an ugly squid like you so fortunate?

OSCAR: Throw worms in her face—works miracles.

FLORENCE: No, Oscar, it's your beautiful eyes.

OSCAR: Ah, but the rest of me...

FLORENCE: (*Teasing.*) You're *interesting*-looking.

OCTAVIA: How do you come to know so much about spiritualism, Mister Doyle?

ARTHUR: Read a book about it, ma'am. Absolute bosh. When we die, we die.

OSCAR: Oh, dear, Bram. Arthur's evolved beyond his soul.

MISS QUIMBY: An acquaintance of mine claims a medium summoned her uncle from the grave.

ARTHUR: And heard spirit knocks, no doubt?

MISS QUIMBY: Absolutely.

ARTHUR: Science proves every medium a patent fraud. Knocking is accomplished with wires and hidden panels. Ectoplasm is quite often merely mucus.

OCTAVIA: Mister Doyle! Pfff!

ARTHUR: My apologies, ladies. I've spent the last year almost exclusively in the company of books and medical lecturers.

FLORENCE: Oscar, when this fakir arrives, do let's send him home and go straight to bed.

OSCAR: Professor Dvapara is a mesmerist, not a medium.

(*Suddenly* TY, *eighteen, an angelic-looking groom, hurtles in through the hall doors in a panic. He is dressed in work clothes and has a scarf wrapped tightly around his neck.*)

TY: (*Cockney*) Mister Wilde, lock the door! The filthy blighter's after me!

OSCAR: Ty, we have guests—

TY: (*Clutching* OSCAR, *much to* OSCAR's *embarrassment.*) A great gamey spider, Mister Wilde! Coming up the drive!

MISS QUIMBY: Shut it, lad! There's people of gentility about.

OSCAR: Calm yourself, Ty.

TY: I ain't lying. Tried to suck the life outta me, it did! (OSCAR *hands* TY *to* MISS QUIMBY.) Don't let it in!

OSCAR: We won't, Ty. (*To* MISS QUIMBY) Please feed him—something soothing.

MISS QUIMBY: Conk him on the head with that linga-thing, that'll soothe him.

TY: (*Desperately, as* MISS QUIMBY *drags him away.*) Promise, Mister Wilde!

OSCAR: Trust me, Ty. (*He turns back to his guests.*) The boy's been overexcited since we came from London. He's very good with the horses, but—

OCTAVIA: Discharge him at once. Most unnerving.

BRAM: Have you seen this mesmerist perform?

ARTHUR: And were you satisfied with his authenticity?

(BRAM *again attempts to pass the note to* FLORENCE, *but she evades him.* BRAM *barely manages to hide the note before* OSCAR *looks at him.*)

OSCAR: Absolutely! Last week—also during the wee hours, I might add—I saw him regress a beautiful barmaid into her previous life as a duchess.

OCTAVIA: Plays havoc, no doubt, with proper genealogy.

ARTHUR: He delivered what she naturally desired: respectability and position.

BRAM: What are you saying, Doyle?

(*Doorbell rings.* MISS QUIMBY *goes out.*)

ARTHUR: These fellows are born showmen—playing on an audience's imagination and secret dreams. Wilde, may I volunteer as subject for this experiment?

OSCAR: Certainly, my dear fellow. If he's successful with a cynic such as yourself, he deserves to take us in.

(OSCAR *hands* BRAM *the napkin of worms. In accepting the worms,* BRAM *almost reveals the note.*)

OSCAR: Here, Bram. See if you can win Florence with these, there's a good fellow.

MISS QUIMBY: (*Entering*) Professor Dvapara.

(BRAM *shoves the note into* FLORENCE's *hand. Angrily, she hides it in her sleeve.* PROFESSOR DVAPARA, *twenty-nine, is a strikingly handsome man who enters the room with an air of utmost elegance. He wears a long, full cape. Although he has an Indian complexion, in speech and dress he is quite European.*)

OSCAR: Professor Dvapara, welcome.

DVAPARA: (*Formal, a la Bela Lugosi, but with no discernable accent*) Good evening. (*He takes* OSCAR's *hand.*) You are looking well.

OSCAR: (*Staring for a moment*) This...is my fiancée, Miss Balcombe.

DVAPARA: Miss Balcombe.

FLORENCE: (*Smiling.*) Professor, I expected someone much older. Wizened with age and experience in these matters.

DVAPARA: Experience does not wizen everyone, Miss Balcombe.

OSCAR: This is Miss Balcombe's aunt, Mrs Octavia Balcombe.

(DVAPARA *bows*.)

OCTAVIA: How charming that your speech is unencumbered by an Indian accent.

DVAPARA: I have seen the world, dear lady. I've found it most convenient to travel light.

OSCAR: And Mister Bram Stoker, soon to be associated with the Lyceum Theater in London, and Mister Arthur Conan Doyle.

BRAM: (*Starts to shake hands, shoves worms in his jacket pocket.*) Dvapara.

ARTHUR: A Naga, are you?

DVAPARA: Proudly, sir, I claim that ancestry. You have heard of my forefathers who defended the Indus Valley against the Mughals?

ARTHUR: And decapitated their enemies to steal their souls. Do you actually believe the soul resides in the head?

OSCAR: Arthur is a medical student.

DVAPARA: Ah. And a skeptic, no doubt?

ARTHUR: Not of genealogy. But I wish to be your first subject tonight.

DVAPARA: (*Smiling*) Very well—a challenge. Please be seated.

(DVAPARA *indicates a chair.* ARTHUR *sits.*)

DVAPARA: I need but one source of light.

(*The others dim the gaslights.* OSCAR *lights a single candle and places it before* ARTHUR *and* DVAPARA. *They all take seats.*)

DVAPARA: I require complete silence and attention at all times. Any sound could break the trance.

ARTHUR: Dvapara, what precisely is your academic discipline?

DVAPARA: Antiquity.

OSCAR: Ah! We are colleagues!

FLORENCE: Darling, please allow the professor to begin before I become involuntarily— (*She yawns.*) Somnambulent.

DVAPARA: I apologize for the lateness of the hour. It is the only time I have found mesmerism truly effective.

ARTHUR: Exhaustion is easily confused with a trance state.

DVAPARA: (*Taking out a coin*) I am deeply appreciative of your reluctance to believe. It will make your surrender infinitely more credible.

ARTHUR: (*Indicating the coin*) Fourth-century Gupta, is it?

DVAPARA: (*Flashing the coin in the light*) Very observant.

BRAM: But it looks newly minted!

DVAPARA: (*Hypnotically*) It is an heirloom given me by my father, and to him by his father, continuing back through generations of Dvaparas to the original Naga tribes. From a time before barbaric races overran us— Aryans, Macedonians, Sakas, Mauryans, and Bactrians.

(*Everyone is extraordinarily attentive.* ARTHUR'*s eyes have begun to glaze over, and* FLORENCE *leans forward in her chair, staring.*)

DVAPARA: My remaining relatives slaughtered by British soldiers in the Sepoy Mutiny of 1857. I have wandered the earth for untold years, endured cruelties beyond the ken of sensate flesh and ecstasies that

would kill an ordinary man. The cultures of the world
are mine, yet I abandoned all to settle on this fair isle—
among an ancient race that would honor my blood.
Soon I will no longer merely mesmerize Englishmen
for their amusement, but live among you as I ought.
Mister Doyle?

(DVAPARA *closes his fist over the coin.* ARTHUR *is
hypnotized.*)

ARTHUR: Yes.

DVAPARA: I want you to remember a time when you
were ten years old. Can you recall it?

(ARTHUR *frowns.* FLORENCE *nods solemnly.*)

DVAPARA: Do you remember before that, when you
were a babe?

(ARTHUR *and* FLORENCE *nod.*)

DVAPARA: You must go back further, inside your
mother's womb, when you were but an homunculus.
And further still, before this life began—before your
previous death.

(ARTHUR *begins to giggle quietly, but foolishly, as if he were
insane. At the same time,* FLORENCE's *body twists into a
distorted position.*)

DVAPARA: Where were you before this life? What are
your thoughts?

FLORENCE: (*Bursts out in a cracked voice, startling
everyone.*) I'm old!!

(*They all turn to* FLORENCE, *but* ARTHUR *keeps giggling
quietly.*)

FLORENCE: I'm hideously ugly! A foolish old woman!
My skin is tortured with wrinkles and they've filled
this cell with mirrors. My lips, once red and full, now
pale and dry. Why must I live as rotting flesh—when
for years I was so beautiful?

DVAPARA: Who are you?

FLORENCE: (*With great dignity*) I am Countess Elisabeth Bathory. Make me lovely again!

DVAPARA: Where are you?

FLORENCE: A wretched prison in Hungary.

DVAPARA: When?

FLORENCE: The year of our Lord sixteen hundred and eleven. I must bathe in beauty to wash away the years! Help me.

DVAPARA: How may we help you?

FLORENCE: Bring girls, young virgins.

OCTAVIA: Florence, this is most indecorous.

FLORENCE: They must be pure, to purify me. To wash away my sins.

OSCAR: Professor, I believe this is quite enough.

FLORENCE: Cleanse me with their blood.

BRAM: I say, sir, put a stop to this!

DVAPARA: Rousing her too quickly could harm her.

FLORENCE: Let me bathe in their blood. My skin needs their youth.

OCTAVIA: Mister Wilde, I beg you!

OSCAR: Professor!

FLORENCE: A warm bath for my face, to soak away the lines of age.

DVAPARA: Countess—

FLORENCE: For my breasts, to make them round and soft—

BRAM: (*Going to her*) Florence, please wake up.

DVAPARA: Gently, Mister Stoker.

FLORENCE: (*Touching him, lustfully*) Are you a virgin? Ah, I can see you are!

OCTAVIA: My dear!

OSCAR: Bram, let me—

FLORENCE: Give me your life.

BRAM: Florence, you are not yourself.

DVAPARA: I warn you, Mister Stoker.

FLORENCE: Give me your blood.

(*Suddenly a horrible scream erupts from the doorway as* TY *steps in and sees* DVAPARA.)

TY: The fiend! You've let it in! The nasty human spider!

(FLORENCE *is shocked out of her trance and clutches* BRAM. ARTHUR *wakes up and looks bewildered.* DVAPARA *turns up a gaslight and* OSCAR *tries to restrain* TY.)

OSCAR: Ty, for the love of God!

TY: Kill it, Mister Wilde, before it catches us all! He's looking at me all hungry-like! (*Clutches* OSCAR) Can't you see what he wants?!

BRAM: Don't listen, Florence!

OSCAR: Outside, Ty, please!

TY: (*As* OSCAR *drags him out into the hall*) Don't let him snare you in his web!

OSCAR: (*Offstage*) Come along!

ARTHUR: (*After a bit of silence*) Stoker, what have I missed?

OCTAVIA: Merely the unfortunate consequences of allowing stable help into the drawing room. My apologies, Professor, in Mister Wilde's stead. Tell me, are you really of royal blood?

DVAPARA: It fills my veins, dear lady.

(DVAPARA *kisses* OCTAVIA'*s hand. She is pleased.*)

DVAPARA: I regret I must leave you now.

BRAM: Not without an apology to Miss Balcombe.

FLORENCE: Bram, whatever for?

DVAPARA: Miss Balcombe's past was only unlocked by mesmerism. I cannot bear responsibility for what is found there. Nevertheless, young lady— (*He kisses her hand. She is pleased.*) I hope you will forgive me if I have inconvenienced you.

FLORENCE: Nonsense, sir. If I've said something dreadful, it's my own fault.

ARTHUR: What has she said? What the devil's gone on?!

OCTAVIA: If you'd only pay attention, Mister Doyle, instead of gibbering in that infantile manner—

ARTHUR: Gibbering?

BRAM: Doyle, let's see Professor Dvapara to the door, shall we?

DVAPARA: I shall be indebted to you, sir. Ladies.

BRAM: Your ancestors were kings, you say?

FLORENCE: Good night, Professor.

BRAM: (*As he,* DVAPARA, *and* ARTHUR *disappear down the hall.*) Professor, I wonder, could you appraise this Buddha for me?

DVAPARA: I am not a Buddhist, sir.

OCTAVIA: (*On her way to the door.*) Florence, I shall ask that in future you avoid mesmerists like the plague and keep your beauty secrets to yourself. (*She leaves.*)

(FLORENCE *goes immediately to one of the French doors and peers out, watching* DVAPARA *depart down the drive.* BRAM *comes in and goes to* FLORENCE, *joining her at the window.*)

BRAM: Have you read my missive?

FLORENCE: Mister Stoker, your persistance is almost as charming as your methods are childish. That is not why I asked Oscar to invite you here. I care only for him.

BRAM: But you stare into the night after Eastern mystics?

FLORENCE: Professor Dvapara has panache. That marvelous cape.

BRAM: I'll get one! (*Taking her hand*) You're becoming as stodgy as your ancient aunt.

FLORENCE: Mister Stoker—

(*Behind them,* MISS QUIMBY *creeps into the room.*)

BRAM: What's attractive about Wilde? He's not good-looking.

FLORENCE: I admire his soul. Now, please. You are Oscar's friend and he trusts you. I must trust you as well because he's introduced me to so few of his other acquaintances—

BRAM: A bad lot—

FLORENCE: Perhaps it's their influence, but his behavior since before we left London has been most disturbing. Uproarious enthusiasm for wild entertainments alternating with crashing despair. (*Takes a small bottle of white powder from her sleeve*) And I found this in his room.

MISS QUIMBY: There's a stalwart gentleman, stealing another's lady!

BRAM: Damn these country homes! There's no privacy. Good night, Florence. We shall speak later. (*He leaves hurriedly.*)

MISS QUIMBY: (*Calling after him*) What do I get to keep me mouth shut?

FLORENCE: (*Hiding bottle*) Miss Quimby, he's harmless.

MISS QUIMBY: Right. And a fine little countess you are! Too precious to touch a worm, but oh, what you'd like to do!

FLORENCE: What did I say? Did you hear? No one would tell me.

MISS QUIMBY: Couldn't help but hear you all throughout the house. Shrieking about taking a bath in blood.

(ARTHUR *comes in quietly.*)

FLORENCE: In front of all those people—

MISS QUIMBY: Worse than that, dearie, you wanted virgin's blood!

FLORENCE: Well, at least *you're* safe.

MISS QUIMBY: Ooo! Here! Got your tongue loosened up now, I'll wager!

ARTHUR: Miss Quimby, please. Miss Balcombe's had an unusual experience, and from what I understand, so have I.

MISS QUIMBY: Ain't we all?

FLORENCE: Forgive me, Miss Quimby. I am feeling a bit queer, as you might imagine. (*She goes to the door.*) Good night, Mister Doyle. (*She leaves.*)

ARTHUR: Good night.

MISS QUIMBY: Cold-blooded as a worm, that one. But some gentlemen like icy ladies, don't they, Mister Doyle?

ARTHUR: (*Embarrassed*) If you don't mind—

MISS QUIMBY: I never mind.

(ARTHUR *can only stare.*)

MISS QUIMBY: What kind of woman do you enjoy, sir? If I may inquire?

ARTHUR: Miss, I...uh...

MISS QUIMBY: Oh, dear me! What a forward girl I am! Let's change subjects, shall we? How old are you, lad?

ARTHUR: Almost twenty.

MISS QUIMBY: (*Stroking the linga*) Compelling little oddity, ain't it? Demands stroking. (*Puts his hand on the linga*) So smooth. Twenty's a pretty age. Cool to the touch, ain't it?

ARTHUR: It's been worn away by centuries of adoration.

MISS QUIMBY: Man of science, are you?

ARTHUR: I...uh...attend medical college at Edinburgh.

MISS QUIMBY: (*Moving closer*) Doctor Doyle, then, is it?

ARTHUR: Not yet.

MISS QUIMBY: Have you had much experience with anatomy?

ARTHUR: Oh, yes, I've dissected several cadavers in various states of decay—

MISS QUIMBY: Oh, no, I'm talking about live anatomicals. Frinstance, I've a terrible swelling right here— (*She places his hand on her bosom.*) —Could you get me some relief for it, Doctor? (*He tries to take his hand away, but she replaces it.*) I'd like a thorough examination, if you don't mind. Praps I should pay a visit to your office later this evening?

ARTHUR: (*Clears his throat*) I'm afraid I'm sharing quarters with Mister Stoker.

MISS QUIMBY: Of course, of course. Mustn't disturb that two-faced bag of wind. I'm in with the cook unfortunately, but there's always the stable. It's warm, the hay smells sweet, and if I drop a copper to Ty and the other stableboy I'm quite sure they'd oblige us and disappear.

ARTHUR: Miss, I must confess you're very...I mean I'm rather...or actually *very* inclined, however...

MISS QUIMBY: What a sweetie! So shy! For you, it's only three shillings.

ARTHUR: Three shillings!

MISS QUIMBY: Usually it's a crown. (*Takes a dainty brandy bottle from her bodice.*) Care for a tipple?

ARTHUR: Consider yourself lucky I do not inform Mister Wilde of your activities. I'm quite certain he would not be pleased—

MISS QUIMBY: He knows. And says not a word. Me regular wages are next to bloody nothing—

ARTHUR: Why, you're inebriated.

MISS QUIMBY: He says not a word and I say not a word. An even exchange.

ARTHUR: Surely you're not accusing your employer—

MISS QUIMBY: He's a nice boy. Very upright and decent. Awfully religious of late, but not a man who ought to get married.

ARTHUR: (*Trying to leave*) Good night, Miss Quimby.

(MISS QUIMBY *produces a syringe.*)

MISS QUIMBY: Doctor Doyle, look what I found peeping out of your medical bag.

ARTHUR: (*Trying to take it*) I'm a doctor! Of course I have syringes—

(MISS QUIMBY *touches her finger to the needle, then rubs it on her gums.*)

MISS QUIMBY: I ain't as ignorant as you might suppose. Every man's got his weakness.

(ARTHUR *takes the syringe.*)

MISS QUIMBY: Praps you've more than one.

(MISS QUIMBY *leaps up and kisses* ARTHUR *full on the mouth. He doesn't actually respond, but she has taken his breath away. After a moment, she pulls back.*)

MISS QUIMBY: Half an hour, then?

OSCAR: (*Offstage.*) Ty, this is intolerable.

(ARTHUR *nods and fairly runs out of the room.* MISS QUIMBY *follows more slowly, smiling.* TY *precedes* OSCAR *into the room, carrying a bundle of blankets.*)

TY: If you'd rather I lose me blooming mind out in the bleeding stable—

(TY *almost runs into* MISS QUIMBY.)

MISS QUIMBY: You've already lost it in here, lad.

OSCAR: Not a word, Miss Quimby.

(MISS QUIMBY *goes.* TY *starts spreading blankets on the settee as* OSCAR *carefully shuts the doors behind them.*)

OSCAR: What do you imagine my guests will say when they find a horseman lounging in the drawing room?

TY: (*Imitating aristocracy in a silly voice*) Oh my heavens! A horseman lounging in the drawing room!

OSCAR: This is a respectable house.

TY: Respectable, is it?

OSCAR: For God's sake, my future aunt-in-law is visiting.

TY: Why'd you want me to meet you in the cemetery tonight?

OSCAR: (*Pause; he is taken aback.*) To propitiate our Druidic ancestors for predictions of the future. A very beautiful churchyard, didn't you find? Nothing there but moonlight and death.

TY: Druids, my arse. I've heard tales about the goings-on in London cemeteries after dark. Does the same hold true in Ireland?

OSCAR: I can't imagine what you mean.

TY: Miss Quimby tells me you've got a *great* imagination. Imagine what happened to me behind that tombstone this evening!

OSCAR: I'd rather not.

TY: Aw, never mind. I'll keep shut about it if you let me stay here tonight.

OSCAR: Ty, I'd like to oblige you—

TY: (*Taking off the scarf, with real fear*) Care to see what actually occurred in the boneyard? Treat yourself to these nasty gashes. Look at my neck! (*Hesitantly,* OSCAR *peers at* TY's *neck.*) You saw the fellow what drug me into that cape of his. Moonlight and death!

OSCAR: Tick bites. From sleeping in the stable.

(TY *begins checking all the doors and windows the make sure they are locked.*)

TY: Biggest tick I ever seen. And you, like a fool, inviting the bloody monster into your house!

OSCAR: Pure xenophobia on your part. Professor Dvapara is a cultured gentleman, albeit of foreign extraction.

TY: He sucked me blood, Mister Wilde. Tried to drain me dry, he did! I almost got murdered to death out there and you run off—saving what? Your reputation? Bloody hell.

OSCAR: Very well. Stay here. But out to the stable in the morning before my guests wake up.

TY: (*Taking* OSCAR's *hand*) Bless you, Mister Wilde. You're a damn fine fellow for a gentleman.

OSCAR: (*Turning off the gaslight*) Good night, Ty. Sleep the sleep of angels.

(*In the darkness,* TY *gasps.*)

OSCAR: Ty, what's the matter?

TY: (*Laughing with embarrassment*) I...ain't been scared of the dark since I was a kiddie.

(OSCAR *lights the candle that was used during the mesmerism.*)

OSCAR: Then, let there be light. And God saw the light that it was good; and God divided the light from the darkness. And God called the light Day, and the darkness he called Night (*He tenderly smooths* TY's *hair.*)

TY: G'night, Mister Wilde.

OSCAR: Remember, fear is a completely useless emotion.

TY: Still, it don't hurt to be careful.

(OSCAR *smiles and leaves.* TY *snuggles down into the blankets and tries to go to sleep, but his eyes refuse to close. Finally, after much tossing and turning, he sings to himself in a sweet, childish voice,* Brother James' Air.)

TY: The Lord's my shepherd, I'll not want
He makes me down to lie
In pastures green he leadeth me
The silent waters by
He leadeth me, He leadeth me
The silent waters by

(*While* TY *is preoccupied with his singing, a mysterious fog seeps in from under the draperies of one of the French doors.*)

TY: (*Sitting up slowly, as if hypnotized*)
Yea, though I walk through shadowed vale

I will fear no ill
For Thou art with me
And Thy rod and staff me comfort still
Thy rod and staff me comfort still...

(*The fog ceases and* DVAPARA *steps out of the draperies, caped and visible only in dim silhouette.* TY *stares at him, mesmerized. Slowly he stands and goes to* DVAPARA, *touching the cape in childish awe. In one swift, smooth movement,* DVAPARA *wraps* TY *in the cape as a mother would a child, or a spider would a fly.* DVAPARA *puts out the candle and in the darkness* TY *gives an erotic cry of despair. Silence for a few moments, then* OSCAR *creeps into the room with a single lit candle.*)

OSCAR: Ty, where are you? Are you quite all right?

(OSCAR *prowls about, searching the room until he comes to the draperies from which* DVAPARA *recently issued forth. He throws them open and gasps when he discovers* ARTHUR *hiding there.*)

OSCAR: Arthur, are you mad?

ARTHUR: I heard a noise, out near the stable, and was on my way to investigate.

BRAM: (*Rushing in with a candle*) What was that dreadful cry? It sounded like a soul in torment.

ARTHUR: (*As* OSCAR *turns up the lights*) It sounded like Wilde's groom—I recognized the vocal modulations.

BRAM: Good gracious, Doyle!

OSCAR: I allowed him to sleep here because he was still frightened.

BRAM: He appears to have declined your offer.

ARTHUR: Or perhaps his fears were realized. Did he enlighten you regarding his terror of Professor Dvapara?

OSCAR: (*Still searching the room*) Well, it seems...oh, never mind. It's late and I may have been slightly mesmerized myself.

BRAM: (*Starting to search as well*) Oh, out with it, Wilde. What chilled him so?

OSCAR: I retreated here for quiet inspiration and instead— (*Laughing with embarrassment*) Have either of you read Varney the Vampire?

(*Outside, a dog howls in the distance.*)

ARTHUR: Oh, rubbish.

BRAM: No, but I've read that vampire story by Polidori.

ARTHUR: I suppose the lad had gaping wounds in his throat and hallucinated bats and wolves?

OSCAR: I don't know if "gape" is quite the proper term, but there were punctures.

BRAM: (*Also searching*) But this is incredible!

(*The search for* TY *continues; they throw open drapes, cupboards, etc.*)

ARTHUR: Pure superstition, gentlemen. Concocted by the Roman Catholic Church to keep everyone wearing crucifixes. Reanimated corpses are easily explained.

BRAM: How is that, Doyle?

ARTHUR: Elementary, my dear Stoker. Epileptic seizures often result in premature burial—such unfortunates are frequently discovered in tortured positions when they are exhumed, having bloodied their lips and fingers tearing at the walls of their wooden prisons.

OSCAR: Oh, how horrid. I'm not sure I wouldn't prefer to believe in vampirism.

ARTHUR: Or soil conditions can preserve a body so that when a stake is driven into the heart of a suspiciously healthy-looking corpse, fresh blood and fluids burst forth.

(ARTHUR *throws open a cabinet, finds nothing. Again, the dog howls.*)

ARTHUR: But, of course, if one can believe in transubstantiation of bread into flesh and wine into blood, every variety of illogic becomes possible.

OSCAR: And what of Christ himself rising from the dead?

BRAM: But not to suck blood from the living.

ARTHUR: In a manner of speaking. But we twiddle rosaries with our thumbs and pray to him, rather than warding him off with wild roses and necklaces of garlic like a proper vampire.

(*More dogs begin to howl.*)

OSCAR: Unrepentent atheist?

ARTHUR: I believe there is an intelligent force in Nature—though to call this force a Galilean seems to me a bit presumptuous. I put my faith in reason, not passion.

OSCAR: Apollo, rather than Dionysis. I worship both.

ARTHUR: And I doubt there is such a thing as a soul that survives death. I've seen little evidence of it in my examinations of corpses and even less in my interactions with the living.

OSCAR: (*Giving up the search*) But how do you explain, my dear Arthur, Ty's absolute disappearance from this room?

BRAM: Why, that's simple logic. He went outside.

ARTHUR: When he was terrified to do so?

(*There is a weak knocking sound at one of the French doors. It grows steadily louder. The dogs stop howling.*)

OSCAR: Perhaps something more horrific was inside.

(*They look about them nervously.*)

BRAM: What's that knocking?

(*They listen as the knocking grows louder, then stare at the curtained French door. None of them move toward it for a moment. Finally* OSCAR *goes resolutely to the drapes and throws them open.*)

OSCAR: Miss Quimby!

(MISS QUIMBY *stands outside the glass, knocking feebly. She looks terrible—paler than death and her eyes wide open but glazed.* ARTHUR *signals frantically behind the other men's backs for her to keep silent.*)

OSCAR: (*Letting her in*) Entre! Entre! You gave us quite a start. Whatever are you doing outdoors in the chill?

(MISS QUIMBY *staggers zombielike into the room.*)

OSCAR: You'll catch your death! Have you seen Ty? He's disappeared.

ARTHUR: (*As* MISS QUIMBY *staggers to the settee and falls upon it*) It's quite apparent she's been drinking—and liable to be incoherent.

BRAM: Wilde, you've not much luck with servants, have you?

OSCAR: (*Going to* MISS QUIMBY *on the settee*) Miss Quimby, shall I help you to your room?

(OSCAR *sits down next to* MISS QUIMBY *and she falls upon him.*)

OSCAR: Oh, dear. This is most indelicate.

ARTHUR: She's drunk herself insensible.

OSCAR: My dear, you're clammy. Arthur, your professional opinion—how may we wake her to trundle her off to bed?

ARTHUR: Must we wake her?

OSCAR: If we carry her down the hall Mrs. Balcombe would undoubtedly pop out of her bedroom and squawk about rendezvous and impropriety.

BRAM: Prick her with a pin. Here. (*Pulls one out of his coat lining, hands it to* ARTHUR) This qualifies as surgery—your field, is it not?

OSCAR: (*As* ARTHUR *reluctantly accepts the pin*) Do hurry, she's not exactly diaphanous.

(ARTHUR *pricks* MISS QUIMBY *in the forearm with the pin. She does not react. He tries again. And again. He quickly jabs her several times with the pin.*)

OSCAR: My dear Arthur, we asked you to prick her, not tattoo her.

(*Panicking,* ARTHUR *reaches up and pulls down* MISS QUIMBY'S *eyelid, then listens to her heart.*)

BRAM: Good God, Doyle, what is it?

OSCAR: Arthur, what's wrong? She's just a bit fermented, isn't she?

ARTHUR: (*Leans back, horrified and saddened*) She's just a bit dead, I'm afraid.

BRAM: No!

OSCAR: How could she—?

ARTHUR: Worse yet, I pricked her several times and found not a single drop of blood.

(*They all stare at each other.* OSCAR *moves away from the body, and the head tilts, revealing two monstrous wounds on* MISS QUIMBY'S *neck.* BRAM *goes to the French door and locks it.*)

OSCAR: A dog—a large dog. I heard one howling earlier.

ARTHUR: (*As he reluctantly examines the body*) Perhaps...
no, the carotid artery is too neatly slashed.

BRAM: Suicide, then?

(*They both just look at him.*)

OSCAR: Do you suppose some diabolical device...using
suction...?

(MISS QUIMBY's *body slides off the settee onto the floor.*)

OSCAR: Oh, dear.

ARTHUR: (*As they all start to pick her up, to* BRAM) Take
her arms.

BRAM: (*Lifting*) Gracious, Wilde, what do you feed your
servants.

OSCAR: (*Holding a leg, as* BRAM *takes another leg, and*
ARTHUR *supports from behind*) Where shall we?

(*They all pull her separate directions, most indelicately.*)

ARTHUR: Back on the settee.

OSCAR: Behind the settee.

BRAM: Out of the drawing room, at least.

(*They freeze when they hear a knock at the hall door. It
swings open, revealing* DVAPARA, *sans cape.*)

DVAPARA: Mister Wilde, your servants appear to be
in the habit of leaving your front door standing open.
(*Surveying the room*) Pardon me—I came in search of
my cape, but apparently this is an inopportune time.
(*Starts to leave*)

ARTHUR: Professor, have you ever seen this young lady
before?

DVAPARA: She admitted me to the premises earlier this
evening.

ARTHUR: Do you notice any change in her appearance
between then and now?

DVAPARA: (*Studies* MISS QUIMBY) When I first made her acquaintance...she was alive.

BRAM: (*Aggressively*) Have you any information as to how she might have been deprived of that fortunate condition?

DVAPARA: Murder, perhaps?

OSCAR: (*Tilting her head to show the wounds*) And what of these?

DVAPARA: (*Looking more closely*) Ah. I've not seen this for years.

ARTHUR: What?

OSCAR: It's familiar?

BRAM: The bite of a vampire, perhaps?

(*The others look at him with pained embarrassment for revealing what they've all been thinking.*)

DVAPARA: (*Smiles charmingly*) Oh, no, gentlemen, these are modern times. Nothing so romantic as that. Although, from my visit to Wallachia I recall the peasants persist in that tragic belief. The violations of corpses they commit in order to rid themselves of nosferatu—

OSCAR: (*Eagerly*) Yes, how do they do it?

DVAPARA: (*Smiles patronizingly*) No, it is too loathsome to describe to gentlemen. This unfortunate creature has been the victim of *coagulum* poisoning.

ARTHUR: What's that? I've never heard of it.

DVAPARA: It is derived from several noxious roots native to Slavonia. In its purest form, a few granules in a major artery produce massive clotting, literally curdling the blood. Such bodies do not bleed.

(*The other three are confounded.*)

DVAPARA: Rather than hunting mythical monsters, perhaps your time would be better spent searching for a more prosaic murderer. Who might have preferred this girl dead? Perhaps she knew some man's darkest secret.

(ARTHUR, BRAM *and* OSCAR *try to appear nonchalant.* FLORENCE *comes into the room through the hall doors.*)

FLORENCE: Gentlemen, will you please retire? I can't sleep at all with this—

(FLORENCE *sees the body; they try to hide it from her.*)

FLORENCE: Camilla! Is she quite well?

(FLORENCE *tries to go to* MISS QUIMBY, *but* BRAM *restrains her.*)

BRAM: No, Miss Balcombe, it's too horrible.

OSCAR: Please dearest, go back to bed.

FLORENCE: (*Breaking free of* BRAM) The poor thing— what's wrong with her? (*Stops when she views* MISS QUIMBY *more closely*) She's dead, isn't she, Oscar?

OSCAR: Yes, I'm afraid so.

FLORENCE: (*Stroking* MISS QUIMBY's *forehead*) You needn't try to hide her from me. Men are always so helpless about death. Women— (*She looks at* DVAPARA, *slightly distracted.*) —Understand it. Or we are, at any rate, more practical about it. Was she attacked? What did she die of?

ARTHUR: Perhaps some queer disease.

FLORENCE: (*Frightened, looks at* OSCAR) Is it contagious?

OSCAR: Please, Florence, go to bed. It's been a long night and we'll tell you about it in the morning.

BRAM: Miss Balcombe, Mister Doyle and I will see you to your chambers.

FLORENCE: (*A bit annoyed, she starts toward the door.*)
As you wish. But don't keep me in the dark, Oscar.
If there's something to be worried about, I'm quite
proficient. Good night, Professor.

(*With looks of caution thrown over their shoulders,* ARTHUR
and BRAM *follow* FLORENCE *out.*)

DVAPARA: (*Amused*) Did you imagine a dead body
would frighten a woman who once bathed in blood?

OSCAR: (*Trying to place* MISS QUIMBY *in a restful position*)
I'm quite sure that was just a nasty thought you placed
in her mind.

DVAPARA: I never manipulate thought. I only call out
thoughts that already lurk within. What lurks within
you, Mister Wilde?

OSCAR: What thoughts did you call out of Ty?

DVAPARA: Ty?

OSCAR: The groom for my horses. The lad who shouted
so when he saw you.

DVAPARA: I've never spoken a word to him.

OSCAR: What of the pricks on his neck?

DVAPARA: (*Smiles*) On a boy his age they could easily
be the marks of love.

OSCAR: (*Embarrassed, he changes the subject*) What *do*
you know of vampires, Professor? Are there incubi and
succubi in India?

DVAPARA: It is certainly an attractive fantasy, is it
not? Quite seductive—eternal life, eternal youth.
Everlasting satisfaction of hungers of the flesh. The
wisdom of antiquity.

OSCAR: Tempting indeed, sir, if one loves life and
thirsts for knowledge.

DVAPARA: When I first saw you, I perceived it. I thirst as well.

OSCAR: To hear Homer recite, or Thespis declaim—

DVAPARA: To inspire Seneca's bloodbaths—

OSCAR: To set eyes on Dante's Beatrice—

DVAPARA: Or Shakespeare's Mister W H.

(OSCAR *looks uncomfortable.*)

DVAPARA: What would one give for such a life? One's soul?

OSCAR: Perhaps. But imagine the shock of Faust attempting to barter his soul and then discovering he never had one—as Arthur proposes.

DVAPARA: (*Moving too close for comfort.*) Certainly you have a soul, Mister Wilde. A soul of genius. I see it dancing there behind your eyes. There's more in you than most men.

OSCAR: That, sir, is mere curiosity, I'm afraid. Ty has disappeared and I believe you know what has happened to him.

DVAPARA: You would do well, Mister Wilde, to refrain from insulting your guests and expend your energies in curbing the immoralities of your servants rather than encouraging them.

OSCAR: (*Frightened and confused by the accusation*) What do you mean?

DVAPARA: (*Gesturing toward* MISS QUIMBY) You see the result.

OSCAR: I resent your intimations, sir. They border on libel. You will understand if I ask you to leave at once. (*Opening the curtains over the French doors*) I believe this is the most direct route.

(TY *is standing outside the window wearing* DVAPARA's *cape. He is so small, compared to the Professor, that it trails upon the ground.*)

OSCAR: (*After a momentary start*) Ty! (*Opens the door*) We've been searching everywhere!

(TY *comes in.*)

OSCAR: And you've stolen the Professor's cape. (*Sotto voce*) Please give it back as he's been most tiresome.

TY: (*Virtually ignoring* OSCAR) I'd give it all back if I could.

OSCAR: Then please do so at once so we can all go to bed.

TY: (*Laughing mirthlessly*) I don't need no sleep. Never no more.

OSCAR: Yes, you do. Now remove that cape.

(OSCAR *tries to take the cape, but* TY *pushes him away effortlessly, sending* OSCAR *reeling.*)

TY: Bugger off. (*To* DVAPARA) You can slink on home, now. He's mine.

OSCAR: Ty— (*He starts toward the hall door.*)

TY: Another step and I'll rip your throat out. Same goes for talking.

(OSCAR *freezes.* TY *sees* MISS QUIMBY.)

TY: Kilt another whore, did you? Easy when they're out at night putting their trust in strangers. Voracious bastard. (*Indicating* OSCAR) I got a prior claim on this one.

DVAPARA: My claim is of centuries. You are weak as a newborn.

TY: Drained me dry, you did. You're obligated to let me fill my veins.

DVAPARA: I owe you nothing.

TY: You love me, in some filthy way. That's an obligation.

DVAPARA: I love you as my creation. Mine to create. Mine to destroy.

(*Outside, a cock crows.*)

TY: The centuries have worn you out. I'm fresh.

DVAPARA: You have no grave.

TY: Cause I never died. And never will.

DVAPARA: (*Bows graciously*) So you believe. Mister Wilde, expect me. (*He disappears.*)

TY: Coward. Afraid of me—can you fathom that? A monster of his caliber—and I put him to flight!

(*To* OSCAR, *who is edging toward the door.*)

TY: But you'll not fly, will you Mister Wilde? Pin you like a butterfly to a card, I will.

OSCAR: (*Edging away as* TY *stalks him.*) Ty, I've always been good to you.

TY: Very good, sir.

OSCAR: Been more than an employer, haven't I?

TY: Much more.

(*Gradually, rays of dawn stream into the room through the open French doors. The light is faint, barely perceptible at first, but grows in strength. Neither* TY *nor* OSCAR *notices it, as their dance of death is around the perimeter of the room and they never step into the pool of light.*)

TY: Careful not to cry out, now. Potentially embarrassing situation, isn't it? In a respectable household.

OSCAR: Please, Ty.

TY: Now *I'm* asking *you* to meet me in the cemetery. Ironical, ain't it?

OSCAR: Do you think it wise to steal the Professor's cape?

TY: Like to see him try and get it.

OSCAR: After all, you're just a boy.

TY: I ain't your boy no more. Your blood belongs to me. Like my blood belonged to him. Stole my life, he did. All the secrets in my blood. But gave me new life. New secrets. The secrets of the ages. Share them with me.

OSCAR: You're not a boy, you're a demon.

TY: And wise as a Druid! Wanna hear me prognosticate your future?

OSCAR: And what happens to demons, Ty? They live in torment.

TY: They take pleasure in torment. Let me torment you, Mister Wilde. You'll love it.

(*They stalk each other in silence for a moment, then suddenly* OSCAR *makes a break for the French door.* TY *almost grabs him as he passes by.* OSCAR *disappears out the door and* TY *starts to follow, but then halts when he steps into the pool of sunlight—as if an invisible hand restrains him.*)

TY: (*Puzzled*) What the hell? (*Looks at his hands in the sun. He gasps, realizing.*) I got no grave. Nowhere to go. Mister Wilde! (*He staggers about the room.*) Mister Wilde, bury me! You owe me that!

(OSCAR *appears in the doorway, hesitant and horrified.*)

TY: I'm on fire! Bury me! The earth is cool. (*Covers himself with the cape*) Take me to the graveyard, Mister Wilde! Don't let me burn. (*Falls to the floor, completely covered with the cape.*) Bury me!

(Smoke begins to pour out from under the cape. TY's screams become inhuman, tortured. OSCAR can hardly bear to watch, but cannot take his eyes away. The smoke billows wildly as TY's screams die away. In the silence, the smoke begins to clear. After a moment, OSCAR goes to the cape and picks it up. There is nothing under it but dust. OSCAR crosses himself and kneels over the cape to pray.)

END OF ACT ONE

ACT TWO

(The next night. The room is virtually unchanged. The only additions are a simple closed casket on trestles and candles and flowers throughout the room. One of the French doors stands open. The room is empty, but after a moment FLORENCE *comes in, followed by* BRAM *and* ARTHUR. *As they speak,* FLORENCE *closes the French door and draws the draperies.)*

FLORENCE: Do you think, Mister Stoker, that you could persuade him to go to bed?

ARTHUR: He hasn't slept in thirty-six hours.

BRAM: *(Alternately gnawing a chicken leg and sipping milk.)* Perhaps, now that the viewing's over and we've all paid our respects—

FLORENCE: *(Trying to take* BRAM's *hands, but they are full of food.)* I'm very frightened. He's worse every moment. *(Takes out the bottle of white powder)* Mister Doyle—

BRAM: Florence, don't—

FLORENCE: *(Showing* ARTHUR *the bottle)* I found this in Oscar's things.

ARTHUR: *(Taking it with a professional air)* Let me examine it. *(Eagerly sniffs contents, is surprised)* Dispose of this at once.

FLORENCE: What is it?

BRAM: Coagulum?

ARTHUR: No, potassium cyanide. Deadly, but the symptoms are nothing like Miss Quimby's.

FLORENCE: What a horrible death.

BRAM: I should have discharged a servant like that at the first sign of ill behavior.

ARTHUR: (*Annoyed*) Oh, yes, Stoker—serves her right.

BRAM: Pardon me, Doyle, I didn't mean— (*Belches quietly*) Excuse me. This stringy chicken's made me a bit queasy.

FLORENCE: (*Gesturing toward the casket*) Mister Stoker, some respect, please.

(BRAM *drops the chicken leg in a wastebasket and sets the half-full glass of milk on the bookcase.*)

ARTHUR: (*Looking at the powder*) This is more frequently an instrument of suicide than an agent of murder.

(OSCAR *bursts in through the hall doors, manically cheerful and laden with a satchel and wreaths of wild roses and garlic.* FLORENCE *snatches the bottle from* ARTHUR *and hides it.*)

OSCAR: (*Hanging wreaths on all the doors and windows*) There's roses, that's for remembrance. (*To* FLORENCE) Pray you, love, remember. And there is garlic, that's for thoughts.

FLORENCE: Paraphrase!

OSCAR: (*Places a wreath around* FLORENCE's *neck*) There's rue for you, and here's some for me. (*Places one around his own neck*) We may call it herb of grace a' Sundays. You may wear your rue with a difference.

BRAM: Rather ungainly for Ophelia, wouldn't you say, Wilde?

OSCAR: But mad enough, wouldn't you say, Arthur?

ARTHUR: Oscar, this is the nineteenth century!

OSCAR: Yes, and I hope to live to the twentieth.

FLORENCE: If we don't all suffocate in this room first. What are you doing?

OSCAR: Protecting us. I'm quite serious—I hope you all realize.

FLORENCE: Protecting us? Oh, yes. Fresh Irish air is quite deadly this time of year. (*Goes to open the French door*)

OSCAR: (*Stopping her*) Leave it closed!

BRAM: Wilde, there's no need to be ungracious.

ARTHUR: If vampires did exist, I'm quite certain they wouldn't be deterred by fragrances.

FLORENCE: Vampires! Oh, Oscar. You're overtired and your imagination's gotten the better of you. Stop talking and go to bed.

OSCAR: It is so exhausting not to talk. Indulge me, please.

FLORENCE: I always indulge you—that's the problem.

ARTHUR: Oscar, I've deduced the solution to the murder and it has nothing to do with vampires.

OSCAR: Coagulum, I suppose?

ARTHUR: Ty himself killed Miss Quimby, then ran away.

OSCAR: Why?

ARTHUR: (*Uncomfortably*) Perhaps some...romantic indiscretion or intrigue.

OSCAR: I have my doubts.

ARTHUR: More plausible still when we remember that Ty tried so desperately to make us think ill of Professor Dvapara.

OSCAR: More plausible still when we recall that Ty was a Slavonian herbalist in a former life and therefore had an intimate knowledge of exotic poisons. Is there such a thing as coagulum, Doctor Doyle?

ARTHUR: I'll admit I've never run across it, but the world holds many secrets even Scottish medical schools are not privy to.

OSCAR: Including vampires. I may not be a man of science, but I did observe with my own eyes—I'm trying to be empirical about this—I saw Ty die because of Dvapara.

BRAM: How?

OSCAR: He was burned to death by the morning sun.

ARTHUR: This is the difficulty of substituting passion for reason.

FLORENCE: How could Professor Dvapara be responsible for that—even if it were true?

OSCAR: Dvapara had vampirized him, turned him into nosferatu—the living dead.

ARTHUR: But what evidence do you have?

OSCAR: (*Producing* DVAPARA's *cape*) This.

(*They just stare.*)

BRAM: That's a cape.

OSCAR: Dvapara's cape. Ty was wearing it when he disintegrated. (*Shakes it. Dust flies.*) That's all that's left of poor Ty.

FLORENCE: Oscar, this is no longer amusing.

ARTHUR: Out of respect for poor Miss Quimby—

FLORENCE: I propose we summon Professor Dvapara and let him vindicate himself. (*Teasing*) Such a handsome gentleman—for a vampire.

OSCAR: Interesting-looking!

BRAM: And return his cape. It's rather fashionable, isn't it, for an import?

ARTHUR: I tried to reach him all afternoon myself, to find out how he made me babble like a fool.

OSCAR: And did you see him?

ARTHUR: Pounded several times on the door of the old rectory to no effect.

OSCAR: See! See! (*He takes out several crucifixes on chains.*) Put these on.

ARTHUR: These relics are childish.

OSCAR: I've toyed with Catholicism for years. Luckily I've saved my playthings.

FLORENCE: (*As* OSCAR *hands her a crucifix*) Oh, Oscar, do you really think he'll return?

OSCAR: He'll come for the cape. He knows it's here.

BRAM: (*Sniffing the cape*) He may not want it after all. It stinks like the grave.

(*They all look at each other and put the crucifixes on, except* ARTHUR.)

ARTHUR: This is absurd. Gods and devils! Besides, he's Oriental—how could Occidental religious symbols harm him?

OSCAR: Christianity is universal salvation!

ARTHUR: (*Indicating the linga*) A stout blow to the skull with this would be more practical.

BRAM: Perhaps he's just the carrier of some tropical plague. Shouldn't we alert someone before it spreads?

OSCAR: We must all stay together in this room. He only attacks those who are alone.

FLORENCE: I'm not about to spend the wee hours of the morning sitting up with a body in a casket.

OSCAR: (*Suddenly quite anxious*) Has one of you been in this room at all times since sunset?

ARTHUR: I believe so.

BRAM: I can't recall leaving.

FLORENCE: Oscar, this is quite enough. I'm going to bed.

OSCAR: Very well. But please leave up the garlands in your bedroom.

FLORENCE: Oh, dear. I'm safe from vampires but will choke to death on the odor of garlic and— (*She sniffs.*)

(*The others look puzzled and sniff as well. They turn toward the casket.*)

OSCAR: No, not already.

(*They resume sniffing and follow their noses to* BRAM.)

BRAM: (*Reaching into his pocket*) Oh, dear, it's the worms.

OSCAR: (*Taking them*) Congratulations all round. We've outlived the worm.

FLORENCE: I feel ill.

OSCAR: (*Dropping the worms in a wastebasket*) Arthur, would you please escort Florence to her room?

ARTHUR: Certainly.

OSCAR: (*Starts to kiss* FLORENCE) Good night, darling.

FLORENCE: Oscar, don't. You reek of spoilt invertebrates.

OSCAR: (*Reaching into his satchel*) The stench will keep me wakeful.

BRAM: I think I'll change jackets. Wilde, you've lost whatever sense you had.

OSCAR: (*Taking out a large knife*) Not my sense of smell.

(*They leave him alone. When they are gone, he hangs a garlic wreath on the decorative horizontal door handles of the hall doors. He sits down, takes a stake of mountain ash from the satchel and begins whittling it. So intent is he on his whittling that he does not notice the door handle begin to jiggle. Finally it jiggles so violently the garlic wreath falls off. The handles rattle loudly enough for* OSCAR *to hear, and he jumps up, crucifix at the ready.* OCTAVIA *comes in carrying her thick book, looking rather bleary, as if she has just risen from sleep.* OSCAR *screams.*)

OSCAR: Back, demon!

OCTAVIA: Mister Wilde!

OSCAR: Oh, Mrs Balcombe! You startled me.

OCTAVIA: A most disrespectful salutation.

OSCAR: (*Returns to his whittling*) My apologies...I haven't slept.

OCTAVIA: Yes, you look it. The events of the day have also rendered me quite insomniac. Therefore— (*Takes out a pad and pencil*) I would like to take this opportunity to put a few questions to you, Mister Wilde, regarding your engagement to my niece. Florence teases you about plagiarism, but what precisely is an aesthetician, or rather, more simply: what do you do?

OSCAR: My dear lady, pray don't degrade me into the position of giving you useful information. We are born in an age when only the dull are treated seriously, and I live in terror of not being misunderstood.

OCTAVIA: Ah. You are an art critic. Pity. But you are young and may outgrow it. What are your religious beliefs?

OSCAR: I must admit, Mrs Balcombe, that my religious convictions have recently been severely shaken. I was raised in a Christian family and I hope to found one. But of late I've been forced to ponder the immensities.

OCTAVIA: Most unfortunate, Mister Wilde. To ponder is to wander.

OSCAR: In this case it's led to whittling.

OCTAVIA: Safe enough. As long as the item you whittle is properly useless.

OSCAR: It possesses a very definite purpose, Mrs. Balcombe. I plan to thrust it into the heart of Professor Dvapara.

OCTAVIA: (*Making a note*) Sense of humor. I was afraid of that.

OSCAR: I'm quite serious, Mrs Balcombe. Professor Dvapara is a vampire and no doubt intends to murder us all. (*Offers a crucifix*) Would you like a crucifix?

OCTAVIA: And a Papist prosletyzer! Mister Wilde, this is most disappointing. Not only do you slander a perfectly respectable gentleman (albeit of foreign extraction), but openly plot to murder him in a most vulgar manner.

OSCAR: It is to save our lives, Mrs Balcombe, yours included.

OCTAVIA: (*Putting away her notebook and rising*) I regard it as an affront, sir, that you consider saving my life without my express permission. As for your vampire theory, it has merely confirmed my suspicions of your unsound mind. Retract it, sir, within twenty-four hours, or acting on behalf of Florence's mother, I shall withdraw her permission for you to marry her daughter. Good night, Mister Wilde!

(OCTAVIA *starts to leave through the hall doors when* BRAM *and* ARTHUR *come in, hiding their crucifixes.*)

BRAM: Wilde, Dvapara's outside.

ARTHUR: But refuses to enter as long as you insult him with these fetishes.

OSCAR: He *can't* enter as long as the roses and garlic are up.

BRAM: (*As he and* ARTHUR *takes down the garlands and hide them.*) Wilde, your behavior is far from gentlemanly and borders on the uncivil.

ARTHUR: The Professor only wishes to pay his respects to Miss Quimby, as is proper. Please remove your crucifix.

OSCAR: Suicide!

BRAM: And that knife.

OSCAR: No!

BRAM: Oscar, this is pure melodrama.

ARTHUR: At least hide it. You're insulting Miss Quimby's memory.

OCTAVIA: You'll never be admitted to the proper social circles at this rate.

OSCAR: (*Takes off the crucifix and puts it in his pocket*) Very well.

(*When they are not looking he hides the knife nearby*)

ARTHUR: Thank you, Oscar. Now you're being reasonable.

BRAM: (*Going to the door*) Professor—he's relented.

DVAPARA: (*Entering the room, somewhat cautiously*) Good evening, Mister Wilde.

OSCAR: (*Grudgingly*) Professor.

DVAPARA: (*Lays his hand on the casket*) Such a tragedy. So young.

OSCAR: Such tempting flesh.

BRAM: Oscar!

DVAPARA: Has the young villain been found?

OSCAR: (*Barely containing himself*) He'll never be found.

DVAPARA: I have reason to believe he stole my cape, as well. I do hope that at least can be recovered.

OSCAR: You value human life less than a cape? (*Grabbing the knife and rushing* DVAPARA) Monster!

BRAM: (*As he and* ARTHUR *restrain* OSCAR) Wilde, you're mad!

OSCAR: How fashionable is a cape on a headless body?!

ARTHUR: (*Taking the knife from* OSCAR) You're just grief-stricken.

OCTAVIA: Professor, we are as appalled as you are. Mister Wilde, let us hope you have recovered your wits by morning. (*She leaves.*)

DVAPARA: (*Calmly*) Good night, madame.

OSCAR: But, he's...he could...oh, dash it all.

BRAM: (*To* DVAPARA) He's actually quite a gentleman.

DVAPARA: The past few days have been a strain for us all.

OSCAR: My apologies, Professor. I've just lost a houseful of servants—you understand my distress.

DVAPARA: Quite well.

OSCAR: (*Producing the cape*) Here, sir. With my apologies.

DVAPARA: Excellent. All is forgiven.

OSCAR: I found it this morning—among Ty's...things.

DVAPARA: (*Taking the cape*) You are indeed a gentleman, sir. (*Suddenly he makes a horrible, violent sound, and jerks back from the cape, holding his hand in pain.*)

BRAM: Wilde, what have you done!

DVAPARA: Fool!

ARTHUR: Oscar, what is it?

OSCAR: (*Revealing the crucifix he had hidden under the cape*) The image of Our Lord! It burns his hideous dead flesh!

ARTHUR: (*Looks at the crucifix, now slightly bent*) Why, it's melted out of shape!

DVAPARA: (*Venomous*) You think good all-powerful? When good and evil battle—both suffer. Until evil triumphs!

BRAM: My god!

OSCAR: You see! He is evil itself!

DVAPARA: Because you wish it, Mister Wilde.

ARTHUR: But there can't be Indian vampires! The Hindoos cremate their dead!

DVAPARA: I was ancient, Mister Doyle, before the first Hindoo was born. But I shall incinerate you all—just as I burned that trinket! (*Sweeping up the cape into his arms*) Beware the night—gentlemen! (*He disappears into the darkness.*)

(*For a moment they are all stunned.*)

ARTHUR: It was a trick, Oscar. Very clever, but sleight of hand. Any fakir could accomplish it with practice. Bram, you're not taken in as well?

(BRAM *silently retrieves the garlands of garlic and roses, replacing them on all the doors and windows.* OSCAR *gathers his weapons: the stake, hammer, and knife.*)

BRAM: How long until daylight?

OSCAR: Hours yet.

BRAM: Shouldn't we keep watch? Or something?

OSCAR: (*Beginning to reel*) Oh, yes. Most definitely. You see, Arthur—the evil proves the good. God can burn the worm—

(OSCAR *starts to fall.* BRAM *catches him.*)

BRAM: Wilde, are you ill?

OSCAR: Relieved, I think. Now that I'm not alone in my madness. Thank you, Bram.

ARTHUR: Can you sleep?

OSCAR: I imagine I shall have to.

ARTHUR: Then I'll take the first watch in here.

BRAM: (*Taking the hammer and ash stake from* OSCAR) I'll look after the ladies.

ARTHUR: Good. Where is your crucifix?

BRAM: (*Putting it around his neck*) Here it is.

OSCAR: Ah! You've come round.

ARTHUR: Scientific curiosity.

BRAM: Oscar, may I see you to your room?

OSCAR: I'd be most grateful. (*To* ARTHUR) Passion over reason, my friend.

BRAM: (*Supporting* OSCAR, *as they leave*) Sorry, old chap, to have been so skeptical. But these are modern times... (*Over his shoulder*) Call me, Doyle, if you should require assistance.

ARTHUR: Certainly.

(*As soon as they are gone,* ARTHUR *replaces the garland on the hall doors. He gets out his medical beg and gives himself an injection. Rejuvenated, he turns down the gas lamps,*

*lights the candle, then glances nervously at the casket. The
dim outline of* DVAPARA *appears outside one of the French
doors haloed in moonlight.* ARTHUR *does not see it. He
reaches into his pocket for the crucifix, but pulls out only
the chain—the cross itself is nowhere to be found. He goes
warily to the coffin. He is about to open it, but stops himself
and takes the garlic wreath from the French door [but does
not see* DVAPARA] *and places it carefully on the casket. He
backs fearfully away from the coffin and pauses before the
French door without a wreath. Steeling himself, he goes to
the casket and does not notice the handle of the unprotected
door begin to move. He lifts the garlic wreath on the casket
and is about to open the lid when he notices the door handle
moving. He leaps to the doors and replaces the garlic wreath.*
DVAPARA's *silhouette disappears. Keeping an eye on the
silhouette,* ARTHUR *goes back to the casket and prepares to
throw open the lid. He realizes he has neither crucifix nor
wreath, and thinking that* DVAPARA *is still outside one set
of French doors, he removes the wreath from the other and
holds it before himself as he flips open the casket. He backs
away, throwing the wreath into the open coffin, but the
coffin is empty. Resting against a wardrobe,* ARTHUR *sighs
in relief. Suddenly* MISS QUIMBY *bursts out of the wardrobe
with a shriek.)*

ARTHUR: Good God!

(MISS QUIMBY *looks like a beautiful monster. Her white
burial gown is stained with blood, as are her lips.)*

MISS QUIMBY: Been waiting for you all night, I have!
Dvapara said you were mine.

ARTHUR: Miss Quimby, I—

MISS QUIMBY: (*Advancing on him seductively*) Left me
out in the cold last night, did you? She's not fit for the
rubbish pile.

ARTHUR: (*Searching about desperately for some defense*) I
assure you—

MISS QUIMBY: You'll see. Tonight you'll get to know me in most intimate detail. Course, I ain't as warm as I woulda been last night.

ARTHUR: (*Seeing the garlic wreath in the casket*) You're not well. You're bleeding. I'm a doctor—let me help you.

MISS QUIMBY: (*Laughs*) I ain't unwell—I'm dead. And I can't precisely call this blood me own, neither. I'll never bleed again. Nor will I suckle babes, but they suckle me. Poor little darlings!

(ARTHUR *starts to move toward the casket;* MISS QUIMBY *intercepts.*)

MISS QUIMBY: Now, now, sir. That's my casket and you're not to molest it. But there is a way you can help me. I'm cold. Give me your warmth, Mister Doyle. Be tender with me. Hold me as you wanted to last night.

(*As if hypnotized,* ARTHUR *touches* MISS QUIMBY.)

MISS QUIMBY: Very nice, Mister Doyle. You'll find it's pleasant being nice to me. I won't charge you nothing this time. All's I ever needed was one good man to turn me round—

(*Just as* MISS QUIMBY *is about to lunge for his throat,* ARTHUR *begins reciting the Latin Mass.*)

ARTHUR: *Kyrie eleison, Christi elison, Kyrie eleison*—

MISS QUIMBY: (*Shrieking, covering her ears*) Shut it! Please, cut it off! I beg you, Mister Doyle!

ARTHUR: (*Rapidly*) *Libera me, Domine, de morte aeterna, in die illa tremenda*—

(OSCAR *and* BRAM *burst in through the hall doors;* BRAM *carries the hammer and the ash stake,* OSCAR *his cross and the big knife.*)

BRAM: (*Dropping the hammer and stake in terror*) Good heavens! She's alive.

OSCAR: (*Brandishing the crucifix*) No, she's not.

(MISS QUIMBY *reels away from him, hissing.*)

MISS QUIMBY: Keep that filthy thing away from me!

(MISS QUIMBY *eyes the door behind* BRAM, *making him very nervous. He looks for a weapon in his pockets.*)

ARTHUR: (*Continuing under*) Quando caeli movendi sunt et terra: Dum veneris judicare saeculum per ignem. Tremens factus sum eto, et timeo, dum discussio neverit, atque ventura ira.

MISS QUIMBY: Mister Stoker, be a love. Let me warm myself.

(MISS QUIMBY *heads toward* BRAM *with outstretched arms but he grabs his Buddha and wards her off with it. She screams.*)

BRAM: *Nom myoho renge kyo! Nom myoho renge kyo!*

(MISS QUIMBY *makes hesitant moves toward each of the exits, but finds her way blocked in each case by religion.*)

MISS QUIMBY: Have mercy!

OSCAR: (*Reciting, overlapping the others*) The Lord is my shepherd, I shall not want. He makes me lie down in green pastures. He leadeth me beside the still waters. He restoreth my soul. He leadeth me in paths of righteousness for his name's sake. Even though I walk through the valley of the shadow of death, I fear no evil; for thou art with me; thy rod and thy staff, they comfort me. Thou preparest a table before me in the presence of mine enemies; thou anointest my head with oil, my cup overflows. Surely goodness and mercy shall follow all the days of my life; and I shall dwell in the house of the Lord forever.

BRAM: *Nom myoho renge kyo. Nom myoho renge kyo.*

MISS QUIMBY: Behave like gentlemen, sirs! I'm just a poor girl!

ARTHUR: *Quando caeli movendi sunt et terra. Dies illa, dies irae, calamitatis et miseriae; dies magna et amara valde. Dum veneris judicare saeculum per ignum. Requiem aeternam dona eis, Domine: et lux perpetua luceat eis. Libera me Domine de morete aeterna in die illa tremenda: quando caeli movendi sunt et terra; Dum veneris judicare saeculum per ignem.*

(MISS QUIMBY *begins making terrified animal noises as they all converge upon her, the ecclesiastical words resounding through the room. She huddles to the floor and eventually takes refuge in her coffin, pulling the lid shut upon herself with a terrible sound. As soon as she is inside, all three men stop speaking and look at each other.*)

BRAM: (*Almost smugly*) The Buddha worked.

OSCAR: Perhaps any symbol of religion—

(ARTHUR *silently picks up the hammer and stake from the floor.*)

OSCAR: Arthur, are you certain?

BRAM: Doyle, perhaps I should—

ARTHUR: (*Firmly*) No. I'll do it. Stoker, be a good fellow and open the casket.

BRAM: (*Tries, can't budge it*) She's gripping it from within.

OSCAR: (*Assisting*) Our Father, who art in Heaven, hallowed be thy name—

(*With a moan from* MISS QUIMBY, *the lid comes off. She sits up, but* ARTHUR *instantly presses the point of the stake to* MISS QUIMBY's *heart, which silences her moan. She sinks back until she cannot be seen inside the casket.* ARTHUR *raises the hammer.*)

MISS QUIMBY: (*Unseen, within the box*) Oh, please, sir. Let me live—if you love me.

OSCAR: Don't listen, Arthur!

MISS QUIMBY: (*Her hands grip the stake*) I know you love me, Mister Doyle. From when you first set eyes on me.

OSCAR: She's lying!

ARTHUR: I can't do it while she's saying these things.

MISS QUIMBY: Because I love you, Arthur. Truly I do. You know I do.

OSCAR: Not a word! Not another word!

(*Desperate, OSCAR takes the knife and hacks at MISS QUIMBY's neck, unseen in the casket. Her words of love drown in a gurgle of blood as her hands flail and grip the sides of the casket.*)

OSCAR: Silence! (*Hacking again; the first blow did not complete the job.*) She doesn't love you, Arthur! She loved them all and not a one! (*Grunting as he hacks again, holding her head still with his hand*) You pitiful, miserable soul!

(*Blood spurts out of the casket onto OSCAR, but he completes the beheading, lifting the severed head slightly out of the casket in the process, then replacing it.*)

OSCAR: Now, Arthur—finish it!

BRAM: For heaven's sake, Wilde, you've already decapitated her.

ARTHUR: Yes, have some pity, Oscar.

(*The disembodied head emits a hiss.*)

BRAM: Oh, my Lord.

MISS QUIMBY'S HEAD: (*Weakly*) Kiss me, Arthur.

(*BRAM steadies the stake as ARTHUR pounds it in with the hammer. The head screams at each blow.*)

OSCAR: (*Rapidly*) The Lord is my shepherd; I shall not want.

MISS QUIMBY'S HEAD: I—

ARTHUR: (*Grunting as he pounds*) You—

OSCAR: He makes me lie down in green pastures.

MISS QUIMBY'S HEAD: —Love—

ARTHUR: (*Blood spurts upon him*) —Filthy—

OSCAR: He leads me beside the still waters.

MISS QUIMBY'S HEAD: —You!

ARTHUR: —Whore!

(*With the final blow, the head screeches and lies still.*)

OSCAR: He restoreth my soul.

(*Overcome,* ARTHUR *holds onto* OSCAR *for support.*)

BRAM: Well done, Doyle. You've burst her heart.

OSCAR: Oh, Bram, do shut up.

BRAM: Why, you loquacious popinjay! Telling me to shut up. I suppose you could have done what Doyle did?

ARTHUR: (*Weakly*) Each man kills the thing he loves.

OSCAR: Surely you didn't love her, Arthur?

BRAM: A common kitchen slut.

DVAPARA: (*Entering through the unguarded French door*) Of course he loved her. Otherwise he never could have driven a stake into her flesh. (*Going to the head*) I understand, Mister Doyle. I loved her as well. (*Kisses the head's lips*) As I love all my children. (*Gently places the head in the casket*) As I love you.

(*When* DVAPARA *turns to them, they all instinctively raise weapons:* BRAM *the Buddha,* OSCAR *the crucifix, and* ARTHUR *the knife.*)

DVAPARA: (*Laughs*) What paltry weapons, gentlemen. My strength grows hourly, the more I feast.

OSCAR: (*Fearful*) On whom, Dvapara?

DVAPARA: Whom do *you* love, Mister Wilde? (*Calls, commandingly*) Countess!

(OSCAR's *eyes widen in terror*.)

DVAPARA: You see my power? You cannot guard all ports of entry.

(*In the tense silence they hear slow somnambulent footsteps. Finally* FLORENCE *opens the hall doors and comes in wearing her nightgown—she stares at* DVAPARA, *hypnotized. There are two small but noticeable holes in her neck.*)

OSCAR: (*Going to her*) Florence!

FLORENCE: (*Straining toward* DVAPARA *as* OSCAR *holds her back*) My love.

DVAPARA: Come to me, my sweet one.

OSCAR: You beast.

BRAM: She's so pale!

ARTHUR: (*Examining her*) Let me see her fingernails.

OSCAR: Preying on the innocent—!

ARTHUR: Wilde, she's dangerously anemic.

DVAPARA: You cannot keep her from me, Mister Wilde. Some night you will leave her side. And when you do—

OSCAR: I'll never leave her.

DVAPARA: Then I will have *you* first.

ARTHUR: Professor, you will not live another night. (*Pulls the stake from the corpse*) I have deduced where you rest during the day— (*Taking the hammer and stake to the French door*)

DVAPARA: No man knows where I lie!

ARTHUR: —And you shall never lie there again! When I return, Wilde, we'll give Florence a transfusion.

(ARTHUR *dashes out through the French door.* DVAPARA *blocks the crucifix with his cape and brushes past* OSCAR *to the door.*)

DVAPARA: He will not return. (*Disappears after* ARTHUR)

FLORENCE: (*Reaching for* DVAPARA *as* OSCAR *restrains her*) My life!

OSCAR: Bram, quickly—the garlic!

BRAM: (*Obediently replacing the garlic on all the doors.*)
Unfortunately, Wilde, this is a bit akin to sealing the cave after the bat has flown.

OSCAR: It's not for him! It's to keep Florence inside.

FLORENCE: He'll return. (*She sits down, still entranced.*)
He'll come for me.

BRAM: We can't just sit here—

OSCAR: I shan't leave her.

BRAM: —While Doyle is out there with that fiend.

(OSCAR *turns back to* FLORENCE, *who sits staring straight ahead. He kneels and kisses her hands.*)

OSCAR: Come back to me, dearest.

BRAM: Wilde, are you listening?

OCTAVIA: (*Bustling in through the hall doors, still with her book*) Florence! This a most immodest hour to be awake!

BRAM: She's ill, Mrs Balcombe.

OSCAR: Oh, rubbish, Bram! Mrs Balcombe, Florence has been bitten by a vampire—Professor Dvapara.

OCTAVIA: That nonsense again! What are those wounds in her neck?

(OSCAR *just looks at her. She crosses herself.*)

OCTAVIA: He seemed like such a pleasant gentleman.

BRAM: Wilde, Doyle could be dead by now!

OSCAR: Bram—

BRAM: (*Picks up the knife*) I'm going after him.

OSCAR: You don't know where he's gone.

BRAM: I'll start with the rectory—

OCTAVIA: First go to that little chapel by the Lough and get some consecrated Host!

(*They all stare at* OCTAVIA *in amazement.*)

OCTAVIA: Wards off vampires. I read about it in a magazine serial.

BRAM: This is what comes of colonizing these wogs. (*He disappears through the French doors.*)

OSCAR: Yes, Bram, now he's colonizing us.

(FLORENCE *laughs an evil, chilling laugh.* OSCAR *and* OCTAVIA *stare.*)

END OF ACT TWO

ACT THREE

(*In the darkness, a sound of hammering.* OSCAR, *hammer in hand, is revealed closing the wardrobe door.* OCTAVIA *finishes dressing the wounds on* FLORENCE*'s neck.* FLORENCE *sits stock-still, her eyes glazed.*)

OSCAR: (*Picking up* BRAM*'s glass of milk*) Are you quite certain this will protect us?

(OSCAR *ceremoniously pours the milk over the linga. The liquid runs through channels in the sculpture slowly enough that he is able to collect the runoff in the glass.*)

OCTAVIA: Siva incarnated himself for the salvation of the world.

OSCAR: A Hindoo Christ?

OCTAVIA: And in the Bhagavad Gita Krishna says, "Whatever god a man worships, it is I who answers the prayer."

OSCAR: (*Realizing*) Perhaps that's why Bram's Buddha repelled Miss Quimby.

OCTAVIA: Europeans are so unenlightened about religion. In parts of the Orient, one can be Buddhist, Hindoo, Muslim, and animist all at the same time. That wet piece of stone's every bit as holy as a piece of the True Cross.

OSCAR: Mrs Balcombe, where did you come across these unorthodox ideas?

(*Shyly,* OCTAVIA *points to her thick book.* OSCAR *picks it up.*)

OSCAR: Isis Unveiled.

OCTAVIA: I'm a Theosophist.

OSCAR: (*Examining the title page*) By the notorious Madame Blavatsky.

OCTAVIA: In a former life I was a Druid. I haven't told Mister Balcombe.

OSCAR: Divining the future with fire-cracked bones?

OCTAVIA: We all have our secrets, you know. That's what makes us Victorian.

OSCAR: Yes, but I never imagined—

OCTAVIA: Pff! Young people assume their elders cultivate illiteracy these days. (*Finishing with the bandages*) There. At least no one will see those dreadful marks.

(OSCAR *strides over to* FLORENCE *and passes his hand before her eyes. No reaction*)

OSCAR: She's worse every hour. (*Reaching into the wastebasket*) Perhaps I can shock her out of it.

OCTAVIA: This is not, Mister Wilde, a case of the hiccoughs.

OSCAR: (*Dangling a dirty worm before* FLORENCE'*s eyes*) Florence. (*She does not react.*) I have a present.

(FLORENCE *finally sees the worm. She eats it.* OSCAR *gasps.*)

OCTAVIA: Oh, Florence!

OSCAR: My darling, how has he corrupted you?

(FLORENCE *begins to choke on the worm.*)

OSCAR: Florence, I'm sorry—I didn't mean—!

OCTAVIA: She's choking, Mister Wilde!

FLORENCE: (*Stops choking, takes a deep breath, breaks the trance.*) Oh, Oscar—

OSCAR: Florence, you've come back to yourself!

OCTAVIA: My child!

FLORENCE: Hold, me Oscar. I feel as if I've been imprisoned behind a glass. I see everything, yet can do nothing.

(OSCAR *takes* FLORENCE *in his arms. She clutches him desperately.*)

OSCAR: Darling!

FLORENCE: It's been dreadful. He came to my window and called me "Countess," spoke of bathing in virgin's blood. I was terrified but couldn't take my eyes from his. They seemed more beautiful than any I had ever seen—

OSCAR: More than mine?

FLORENCE: You have beautifully poetic eyes, Oscar. His were beautifully...demanding. Perhaps he never spoke at all—I just saw into his mind through those deep dark eyes. And he saw into mine—into my soul as if he'd torn away a veil. I saw myself as he saw me. (*She gasps and closes her eyes.*) I let him in, Oscar. I feel almost as if I've been unfaithful to you.

OCTAVIA: Ridiculous, Florence.

OSCAR: No, no. You were interfered with. He stole your will.

FLORENCE: He's coming back, Oscar. My blood can feel him coming. (*She gasps again, begins to cry.*) My blood wants him—it's burning me from within. Quickly, Oscar, go to my room. The priest that was here for Miss Quimby left me a vial of Holy Water.

OSCAR: If he's coming I can't leave you!

FLORENCE: Neither can you save me if you stay. Your soul is innocent, Oscar, and young. He is older than Stonehenge, older than anything we know, and has the strength of ages. But God's Holy Water can burn even him! (*She gasps.*) I feel him. I'm losing myself to him.

(OSCAR *hesitates. Desperately* FLORENCE *pulls his face to hers.*)

FLORENCE: Are you lost to him already? Dearest—no! (*Studies his eyes*) You are!

OSCAR: What do you mean?

FLORENCE: How can that be? Without even touching you—he owns you!

OSCAR: That's not true! Kiss me, darling, and you'll see!

FLORENCE: (*Holding him back*) Oscar, no, I see him in your eyes!

OSCAR: You're mistaken! You should only see yourself in my eyes.

FLORENCE: If you seek death, do not choose him.

OSCAR: How can you—? I don't seek—

FLORENCE: (*Takes out the bottle of potassium cyanide*) Take this instead. I'm sure it's kinder.

OSCAR: (*Grabbing it from her, and hiding it*) Where did you get that?!

FLORENCE: (*Despairing*) We are all lost if you are lost. You cannot help me now.

OSCAR: Trust me, I will! Where in your room have you hidden the Holy Water?

OCTAVIA: She's slipping away, Mister Wilde!

OSCAR: Where, Florence?!

FLORENCE: In the— (*She gasps. Then, sadly:*) I cannot love you anymore.

OSCAR: Where?!

FLORENCE: (*With great effort*) In the chamberpot! (*She faints.*)

OCTAVIA: Oh, Florence! (*Goes to her*)

OSCAR: Is she—?!

OCTAVIA: She's merely fainted. Hurry, Mister Wilde. I'll care for her.

OSCAR: (*Going to the door*) I won't be gone a minute. Don't let anyone in—even Mister Stoker or Mister Doyle. Who knows what may have happened to them out there. Trust no one. I'll knock on the door— (*He demonstrates a secret knock.*) Keep it locked and leave the wreath on until you hear that knock.

OCTAVIA: Yes, yes. If we must be adolescent, we must. Please go!

OSCAR: The chamberpot—clever girl!

(OSCAR *goes out, closing the door behind him.* OCTAVIA *locks it and replaces the garlic wreath.*)

OCTAVIA: Florence—

(FLORENCE *sits up instantly, staring straight ahead with a ghastly smile on her face.* OCTAVIA *gasps.*)

FLORENCE: He's coming, aunt. My lover is coming.

OCTAVIA: He is your *fiancé*, Florence. Please speak properly.

FLORENCE: You'll enjoy him, aunt. Everyone does. Inevitably.

OCTAVIA: I'll enjoy him infinitely more when he returns with the Holy Water.

FLORENCE: (*Emits a hissing sigh*) Not—that frustrated poet—Dvapara. (*Angrily*) This room is a Turkish bath! Open a door, you foolish old hag!

OCTAVIA: I realize you are delirious, but do not speak to me in that tone.

FLORENCE: A window!

OCTAVIA: I'm perfectly comfortable at this temperature, thank you.

FLORENCE: These fumes—they're foul! Hideous garlic—this is Ireland, not Italy!

OCTAVIA: I'm beginning to quite enjoy it, actually.

FLORENCE: And roses! Such an oily scent. Throw them out, aunt.

OCTAVIA: I would as soon throw out a Tudor rose. I'm not so easily tricked as that, young lady. I have noble blood in my veins—

(FLORENCE *turns to look at her, almost hungrily.*)

OCTAVIA: —Somewhere back there...

(*The secret knock is sounded at the door.* FLORENCE *and* OCTAVIA *both freeze.*)

FLORENCE: Answer that, will you, aunt?

OCTAVIA: (*Going to the door*) When you have quite recovered, I promise you a serious discussion about your ill manners. (*Opening the door*) Oh, Mister Wilde, at last. Florence has been most rude—! (*But no one is there.*) Mister Wilde? He's gone.

(*When* OCTAVIA *is turned toward* FLORENCE *a bat flies by in the hallway;* OCTAVIA *does not see it.*)

FLORENCE: Go into the hallway, aunt. Perhaps he is hiding.

OCTAVIA: Ah. That would be like him. (*Goes into the hall. Offstage:*) Mister Wilde! Do make an appearance.

(*The bat flies by in the direction* OCTAVIA *has gone.*)

OCTAVIA: The occasion does not call for whimsy! Mister Wilde! (*Returns and sits next to* FLORENCE) I refuse to wander the halls exposing my throat while your Mister Wilde lurks about no doubt giggling to himself.

(*As she speaks,* OCTAVIA'*s enormous puff of hair twitches slightly, but she does not notice.*)

OCTAVIA: I believe I have been most restrained in my behavior toward him thus far, but Florence, I will not permit you to marry a man who is in the habit of admitting vampires to his home. Imagine the scandal! Vampires have such unfortunate connotations—I'm well aware of them. All that suction and the repugnant habit of sleeping in the earth.

(*Although neither* OCTAVIA *nor* FLORENCE *notices, the twitches are soon accompanied by a thin trickle of blood that runs out of* OCTAVIA'*s hair and down her face.*)

OCTAVIA: Could easily be construed as a social indiscretion. No well brought up girl becomes a vampire, Florence. Remember that in case you have any notion of doing so. Now I know there are attractions—I'm aware of those as well. That delicate pallor is rather alluring—but you'd never be able to see it because you wouldn't cast a reflection. Eternal youth must also be quite enticing—even I have on occasion wished to turn my silver back to gold. (*Touches her hair*) But as you grow older you will see youth as the folly it is. Imagine committing the follies of youth for thousands of years—quite tedious in the end. But of course there is no end. Nothing but ingesting other people's blood for centuries and centuries. Think of that, Florence! Blood, blood, blood, and never a decent cup of tea!

(OCTAVIA *puts her hand to her hair, and glancing at it, discovers the blood running down her face. She shrieks.* FLORENCE *just sits there smiling.*)

OCTAVIA: (*Fighting with her hair*) I'm bleeding, Florence! Something's in my hair! (*She gets up, flailing.*) It's lacerating my scalp and won't let go! Help me, Florence! Please! (*Staggers toward the door*) My hair's being torn out by the roots! (*Opening the door*) Mister Wilde! Help me, someone! Lord Siva save me! (*Runs off down the hall*) Mister Wilde! (*One last scream and then silence*)

(FLORENCE *sits smiling for a moment, then gets up and removes the garlic wreath from one set of French doors. She opens the door and goes outside. Moments later,* OSCAR *rushes into the room from the hall, carrying the vial of Holy Water.*)

OSCAR: Mrs Balcombe, I heard—! (*He sees that no one is there and peers down the hall.*) Florence, darling! (*Knocks the secret knock*) I've brought the Holy Water. Ladies, this is distinctly unamusing. (*He sees the open French door.*) My God! (*Runs to it*) Florence! Mrs Balcombe! (*Peers outside, calls*) Florence! No!

(OSCAR *starts to run out, then reconsiders. He puts down the vial and searches the room until he finds what he is looking for: a long scarf, the same one* TY *wore. He wraps it tightly around his neck and starts to run out again. He reconsiders, stops, retrieves the Holy Water and is about to dash out when he almost runs full-tilt into* FLORENCE, *who appears in the doorway.*)

FLORENCE: (*No longer somnambulent*) Oscar!

OSCAR: Florence, you're safe! (*Closes the door behind her*) Have you gone mad? Why did you go outside?

FLORENCE: To follow Aunt.

OSCAR: Why did she go outside? I thought she understood.

FLORENCE: Something got in her hair, Oscar. It was horrible. I tried to find her, but...

OSCAR: Oh, dear.

FLORENCE: Oh, Oscar, forgive me!

(FLORENCE *rushes to* OSCAR's *arms.*)

OSCAR: (*Stopping her at arm's length, suspiciously*) Florence—how long were you outdoors?

FLORENCE: Not more than a few minutes, and that was too long!

OSCAR: Did you meet anyone out there?

FLORENCE: (*Realizes. Laughs*) Oh, Oscar. How silly.

OSCAR: I'm sorry, Florence. But one can't be too careful.

FLORENCE: Yes, if you want to kiss me, perhaps you should decapitate me first.

OSCAR: (*Laughs, embarrassed. Puts down the vial. Goes to her*) Dearest, please accept my apologies.

FLORENCE: (*Keeping him at arm's length*) One moment. Where have *you* been?

OSCAR: (*Astonished*) Why, in your room—as you instructed!

FLORENCE: You've been gone quite a while.

OSCAR: You told me you'd hidden the Holy Water in the chamber pot, but neglected to mention where you'd hidden the chamber pot.

FLORENCE: (*Laughs, embarrassed*) Oh, dear.

OSCAR: I've had no time to become infected.

FLORENCE: (*He holds out his arms to her.*) Why are you wearing that scarf around your neck?

OSCAR: Florence, this is absurd!

FLORENCE: I agree. Simply remove the scarf.

OSCAR: No!

FLORENCE: What a pair! A fine marriage we'll have if we can't trust each other.

(FLORENCE *and* OSCAR *stare at each other—it is a standoff.*)

OSCAR: Recite a Bible verse.

FLORENCE: Pick up that wreath of garlic on the door.

OSCAR: After the verse.

FLORENCE: "And he took a cup, and when he had given thanks he gave it to them, saying, "Drink ye all of it; for this is my blood of the covenant, which is spilled for many for the remission of sins."

OSCAR: Paraphrase!

FLORENCE: Pick up the wreath!

(OSCAR *marches to the hall doors, hesitates a moment, then picks up the wreath.* FLORENCE *smiles and relaxes, holding out her arms.*)

FLORENCE: There. Now that we've both been tested—

(OSCAR *suddenly throws the wreath to* FLORENCE. *She catches it quite expertly in both hands and stands looking at him.*)

OSCAR: (*Humbly apologetic*) Oh, Florence! I'm disgusted with myself.

FLORENCE: (*Setting down the wreath, understandingly*) Trust no one, Oscar.

(FLORENCE *and* OSCAR *go to each other with extended arms. At the last second he grabs her by the wrists and examines her palms—which are a bright, bloody red where the garlic has burned them. She snarls.*)

OSCAR: Garlic burns you! You are his!

FLORENCE: (*Suddenly vicious and animalistic*) And you are mine!

(*As* FLORENCE *and* OSCAR *grapple, he rips the bandage away from her throat, revealing two large, ugly wounds.*)

OSCAR: Stay away from me, Florence, if you've a drop of humanity left in your veins—!

FLORENCE: Men never understand blood. I want more than a drop, Oscar. Let me kiss your beautiful white throat.

OSCAR: (*With all his strength, he manages to push her away*) You'll never kiss me again.

FLORENCE: (*Still confident*) Yes, I will, my dearest. I know why you hide here in Ireland. Face the truth about yourself, Oscar!

OSCAR: What truth?

FLORENCE: One pitiful poetry prize—is that the extent of your genius?

OSCAR: (*Somewhat relieved*) You'll not seduce me with insults—

FLORENCE: Can you only criticize, but not create? You fear that truth more than death.

OSCAR: Filthy creature!

FLORENCE: Would you rather die than not live up to expectations?

OSCAR: I confess—!

FLORENCE: (*Grabbing the bottle from his pocket*) A romantic early death by potassium cyanide!

OSCAR: —I am not an artist!

FLORENCE: Then become one. (*Swallows the bottle's contents, then opens her arms*) To love life, an artist must embrace death. You must lose your life to save it.

OSCAR: You are quoting out of context. (*He grabs the vial of Holy Water.*) The Holy Water, Florence. Do you still want it?

FLORENCE: (*Commandingly*) Pour it out. I no longer serve petty gods.

(OSCAR *gasps as against his will he uncorks the vial and spills the contents on the floor.*)

FLORENCE: Imagine, Oscar. I'll never be a decrepit crone like my aunt. Youth and power—forever!

(*Suddenly* OSCAR *makes a break for the hall doors. He gets just barely into the hall, then freezes. He backs into the room slowly,* DVAPARA *following grandly.*)

DVAPARA: (*Without looking at* FLORENCE, DVAPARA *points at her.*) Be gone.

FLORENCE: He is mine!

DVAPARA: He is mine since before you were mine.

FLORENCE: He belongs to me because he burns for me.

OSCAR: I belong to myself.

(*The vampires begin to laugh.*)

OSCAR: I am not a lamb for your slaughter.

DVAPARA: No man belongs to himself. He is slave to his desires.

FLORENCE: His hungers. You hunger for me, Oscar.

DVAPARA: No, he does not. I know his passions.

OSCAR: Neither of you know me. I am human and you are not.

FLORENCE: I was.

DVAPARA: I understand human yearnings. Your desire for death. A man collecting worms in a cemetery—

OSCAR: As a joke! To laugh at death—you understood that, didn't you, Florence?

FLORENCE: If I can prove that he loves me, will you let me have him? He's of no use to you if he loves me instead.

DVAPARA: True. He would give me no pleasure then. I want his soul, not only his blood.

OSCAR: My soul is not to be bargained for.

FLORENCE: There'll be no bargaining, Oscar. You thirst for me and I thirst for you. It's very simple, isn't it?

OSCAR: (*Backing away toward the glass of milk on the table*) You are no longer Florence—I can't even call you by that name. You're not a woman anymore.

FLORENCE: No, I'm something more wonderful still. How can you resist me now after desiring me for so long?

(OSCAR *has reached the table with the glass of milk on it. He turns his back to* FLORENCE *and sees it.*)

FLORENCE: Poor darling, I've denied you so much.

OSCAR: (*Quietly picking up the glass of milk*) Yes.

FLORENCE: I was cold to you before. Let me be warm with you now.

(FLORENCE *caresses* OSCAR's *shoulders. He shivers.*)

FLORENCE: A tender kiss is all I ask. Please, Oscar.

OSCAR: I am yours.

FLORENCE: (*Turns to* DVAPARA) Do you concede?

(*While* FLORENCE *is turned toward* DVAPARA, OSCAR *pours the milk into his mouth.* DVAPARA *sees this.*)

DVAPARA: (*Bowing slightly*) You have won what you deserve.

(FLORENCE *turns to* OSCAR *and he to her. She grasps the back of his head, pulling his mouth to hers.*)

FLORENCE: At last, my love.

(*As* FLORENCE's *and* OSCAR's *mouths meet, he grasps the back of her head as well. They force their lips together violently. He spews the milk into her mouth. When she realizes what he is doing, she tries to push him away, but he manages to hold her there for a moment longer. Finally she pushes free with a blood-curdling shriek.* DVAPARA *remains impassive, immobile.*)

FLORENCE: Consecrated poison! (*She coughs and chokes.*) Your kiss is venom to me. Sacrament of death!

OSCAR: Of life!

FLORENCE: (*Shrieking*) I'm burning—from within!

OSCAR: (*Horrified, but trying to stay in control*) Florence, I did love you—while you lived. I cannot watch you die.

FLORENCE: (*Staggering to* DVAPARA) Help me. You who gave me life.

DVAPARA: Burn. You were foolish to trust him.

FLORENCE: It is hellfire! Please!

(FLORENCE *reaches for* DVAPARA, *but he pushes her violently away. She falls upon the settee.*)

FLORENCE: You have damned me! Both of you! Damned me with your love, Dvapara! (*She turns her face away, hiding it in the settee as smoke issues from her mouth. In a final, agonizing scream*) Oscar!

OSCAR: (*Overcome, he starts toward her.*) Florence!

DVAPARA: (*Preventing* OSCAR *from going to her*) Do not. She will burn you as well.

(*A dying moan escapes* FLORENCE's *lips in addition to the smoke.*)

DVAPARA: Pity is a fatal emotion.

OSCAR: (*His face in his hands*) Florence. Oh, darling...

(FLORENCE *is quiet and the smoke abates. Silence for a long moment, then* OSCAR *slowly turns to* DVAPARA, *who smiles at him.*)

DVAPARA: What weapons have you left?

OSCAR: None. (*Goes to* FLORENCE, *cradles her in his arms*) Does it give you pleasure, to destroy such beauty? To desecrate purity?

DVAPARA: Yes. It is the most profound pleasure imaginable. Did you not feel it as you immolated her?

OSCAR: Horror is all I felt.

DVAPARA: Ecstasy, is it not? You see, I do have human emotions.

OSCAR: To corrupt the innocent—when there is no reason—

DVAPARA: (*Staring into* OSCAR's *eyes*) Innocence is reason enough. (*Taking* OSCAR's *hand*) Now you understand me...Mister Wilde? The innocent as well as the guilty are mine, but the innocent give me much more satisfaction.

OSCAR: (*Fighting hypnosis as* DVAPARA *draws him closer*) Who gives you this right—?

DVAPARA: Death takes all. That is my right—given to me by every living soul. The woman and the man. The old and the young. The quick...become the dead.

OSCAR: (*Realizing*) And taking life—you never die.

DVAPARA: Exactly, my child. How can death die?

OSCAR: And yet you also give life.

DVAPARA: (*Caressing* OSCAR) Eternally. You are very handsome, Mister Wilde.

OSCAR: No, I'm not at all.

DVAPARA: Your soul has beauty. And beauty is a form of genius—is higher, indeed, than genius, as it needs

no explanation. (*He opens* OSCAR's *shirt.*) But there
will come a day when your face will be wrinkled and
wizen, your eyes dim and colorless, the grace of your
figure broken and deformed.

OSCAR: All men age.

DVAPARA: You will degenerate into a hideous puppet,
haunted by the memory of passions you feared, and
the exquisite temptation you had not the courage
to yield to. I offer youth, youth! There is absolutely
nothing in the world but youth!

OSCAR: (*Weakly*) Knowledge...

DVAPARA: (*Opens his own shirt*) Of good and evil?
Neither exists. Only life...and death. Not one blossom
of your loveliness will fade. Not one pulse of your life
will ever weaken. (*Cuts his own chest with his fingernail;
blood seeps out.*) I offer you the secrets of centuries.
The whispered intimacies of Sappho's bedchamber,
Chaucer's last unfinished poem, the identity of
Marlowe's murderer. I have drunk of their lives and
offer them to you.

OSCAR: (*Almost somnambulant*) Plagiarist...

DVAPARA: They all made love to death. There are
other promises of everlasting life—but are they as sure
as mine? (*Grasps the back of* OSCAR's *head*) Do this in
remembrance of *me*.

(DVAPARA *forces* OSCAR *to drink the blood from his chest.*)

DVAPARA: You never need fear the grave or worms
again. In triumph you will make the grave your home,
and the worms your slaves. Five millenia I have
searched for *you*. (*Pulls* OSCAR's *head back.* OSCAR's *lips
are bloody.*) We are brothers in blood—forever bound to
one another.

(OSCAR *is quite hypnotized.* DVAPARA *rears back his head
to bite—showing his fangs for the first time—and plunges*

his teeth into OSCAR*'s neck.* OSCAR *gasps and reacts
sensually, arching his back and releasing an ecstatic sigh.
Suddenly* ARTHUR *and* BRAM *dash into the room through
the hall doors.*)

ARTHUR: (*As he spies the garland from the hall doors*)
Quickly, Stoker, the garlic.

BRAM: (*Seeing* FLORENCE, *he goes to her*) Florence! My
God!

(DVAPARA *snarls and lets* OSCAR *slip unconscious to the
floor.*)

ARTHUR: The wreath! Bram! Now!

(BRAM *throws it to him and he quickly replaces it on the
door.*)

DVAPARA: (*Laughing as* BRAM *and* ARTHUR *raise
crucifixes*) Mister Doyle, your addiction has made you
a gibbering madman in this life as well! These trinkets
can no longer hold me. After tonight's feast I am
omnipotent!

(DVAPARA *gestures and the crucifixes fly from their hands.*)

BRAM: (*Holding* FLORENCE) Florence.

ARTHUR: Oscar, are you all right?

(OSCAR *manages to moan.*)

DVAPARA: He is mine. You are too late. Today he will
share my grave.

BRAM: (*Looking up with tear-stained eyes*) You have no
grave.

ARTHUR: And you shall not escape this room.

DVAPARA: I will leave this room—after I have anointed
it with your blood.

BRAM: But where will you go?

ARTHUR: Your grave is no more.

DVAPARA: You could not have found it.

ARTHUR: That is chalk on your shoes, isn't it Professor?

DVAPARA: (*Looks at his shoes. There is a whitish substance on them.*) What of it?

BRAM: Doyle noticed it earlier.

ARTHUR: It bears a remarkable similarity to a small chalk cliff we passed as we drove by the Lough on our way here.

DVAPARA: This county abounds in chalk cliffs.

BRAM: Very few of them abut peat bogs.

ARTHUR: Which have a distinctive odor reminiscent of your cape.

DVAPARA: The bog and the cliff parallel each other for miles.

ARTHUR: But there is only one Neolithic circle of stones where the bog meets the cliff.

BRAM: And it was very clear where the ground had been recently disturbed—

ARTHUR: Which led us to a mahogany sarcophagus full of earth in a hollow beneath a fallen monolith.

BRAM: That casket lies in splinters.

DVAPARA: (*After a pause*) With but a handful of that earth I can make any grave my own.

BRAM: Even when that earth is thoroughly mixed with— (*He takes out a Host.*) Consecrated Host?

ARTHUR: We've scattered them all over the monolith as well.

DVAPARA: Where did you find those biscuits?

BRAM: I took them from that little church on the road near the Lough.

(ARTHUR *begins edging toward the linga.*)

DVAPARA: (*Advancing upon* BRAM, *who holds up the Host in defense*) And how did you enter the sanctuary?

BRAM: I broke a window and crawled inside.

DVAPARA: (*Plucking the Host from* BRAM'*s hand*) You stole this.

BRAM: (*Astonished*) Yes.

DVAPARA: Stolen sacraments are no longer consecrated. This is merely bread, not body. (*He eats it.*) Given for you. My grave is still my own.

ARTHUR: (*Rushing him with the linga*) But you must reach it first!

DVAPARA: Enough!

(DVAPARA *gestures toward* ARTHUR. *The mere gesture slams* ARTHUR *backward against the wall.*)

BRAM: (*Rushing* DVAPARA *with his Buddha*) Die, fiend, for Florence!

(*With a mere glance at* BRAM, DVAPARA *sends him reeling backwards.* DVAPARA *turns toward* OSCAR.)

DVAPARA: Come, Mister Wilde. Let your friends witness our consummation.

(DVAPARA *gestures toward* OSCAR, *who suddenly rises to his feet against his will.*)

ARTHUR: No, Oscar. Religion has failed! You have only your will!

BRAM: He is death!

DVAPARA: For him, I am life. Come.

OSCAR: (*Walking toward* DVAPARA *but fighting the force*) You...have murdered Florence.

ARTHUR: Oscar, *you* decide your fate! Reason, not passion!

OSCAR: You have murdered me.

DVAPARA: I have not murdered you. We are one.

OSCAR: And you have murdered yourself. (*Reaches* DVAPARA) Your appetites have betrayed you.

DVAPARA: (*Grabbing* OSCAR *by the hair, forcing his head back*) What foolishness is this?

OSCAR: (*Smiles*) The day of judgment is upon us.

ARTHUR: Morning is breaking, Dvapara!

BRAM: The sun is rising by now.

DVAPARA: (*Smiles, but is nervous*) That is absurd. There's been no cockcrow.

OSCAR: That's because we ate the cock for dinner last night.

BRAM: A dreadfully tough bird.

DVAPARA: (*Hurling* OSCAR *across the room*) Fools! You have made matters that much worse for yourselves. (*Runs to the hall doors*) When next the sun goes down—!

ARTHUR: The earth will sleep peacefully once more.

DVAPARA: (*Seeing the wreath on the door, he hisses.*) Garlic!

BRAM: For you will no longer corrupt its face!

DVAPARA: (*Dashes to one set of French doors*) You cannot imprison me! (*Sees another wreath*) No!

OSCAR: You have imprisoned yourself. When a creature lives in darkness—

DVAPARA: (*Going to the other set of French doors*) I shall burst this room asunder!

OSCAR: —Eventually its eyes atrophy.

DVAPARA: (*Sees the wreath on that door as well*) Remove this contagion!

OSCAR: Destroy this room, destroy us all—you shall die here with your victims!

DVAPARA: (*Roaring*) Remove it!

(DVAPARA *gestures toward* OSCAR, *who goes to the French doors quite involuntarily.*)

ARTHUR: Fight him, Oscar! His power is weakening!

DVAPARA: Go!

BRAM: Don't let him control you!

DVAPARA: Take it off.

OSCAR: No! (*Fighting the urge, he reaches toward the wreath.*)

BRAM: Stop, Oscar!

DVAPARA: Now!

OSCAR: (*Reaching the wreath*) I can't...help myself. (*Tears the wreath off the door*)

ARTHUR: No!

DVAPARA: (*Starts toward the door*) Open it.

OSCAR: Very well.

DVAPARA: I shall return for you tonight. Only the night can be trusted—for it returns faithfully.

OSCAR: As does the day!

(OSCAR *throws open the long, thick drapes and strong morning sunlight streams into the room.* DVAPARA *is knocked backward in midstride by the burning rays.*)

DVAPARA: (*With a hideous, inhuman cry*) Hellfire!!

OSCAR: No, the rays of heaven! God's love!

(DVAPARA *writhes in agony, screaming.*)

DVAPARA: No-o-o-o! Close it! It scalds my flesh!

(BRAM *and* ARTHUR *stumble forward, as if breaking free of* DVAPARA's *power.*)

BRAM: Burn, monster!

ARTHUR: Suffer as you have made others suffer!

DVAPARA: Brimstone in my veins! You cannot burn me out of you!

OSCAR: The sun that gives us life, gives you death!

(OSCAR *throws open the wardrobe. The inside walls have been covered with icons of myriad religions. The three of them grab the weakened* DVAPARA *and thrust him into the wardrobe.*)

DVAPARA: You destroy my knowledge with my power!

ARTHUR: (*Slamming shut the doors of the wardrobe*) There is no hiding from the light of truth!

OSCAR: It purifies the soul!

DVAPARA: Centuries die with me! Sappho's secrets! Marlowe's murderer!

OSCAR: You!

DVAPARA: (*From within the wardrobe*) But I am with you forever in your blood! (*He gives a final wailing cry as smoke billows forth.*)

(*Silence as the cry ceases and the smoke begins to abate.* OSCAR, ARTHUR, *and* BRAM *stand staring. Suddenly,* OCTAVIA *bustles in through the haze, her hair bloodied and tumbling down around her shoulders. It has turned a youthful gold color.*)

OCTAVIA: Oh, this dreadful smoke! How I abhor cigars! If we had proper help they would freshen this room on a regular basis. Where have all the servants gone?! (*She goes to the wardrobe.*)

OSCAR: No, Mrs Balcombe!

ARTHUR: Don't!

BRAM: Please!

(OCTAVIA, *ignoring them, throws open the wardrobe.*
DVAPARA'*s charred skeleton falls out on top of her. She*
screams and falls to the floor. The men all rush to her aid.)

OSCAR: Mrs Balcombe, I asked you not to—

BRAM: Are you quite well?

ARTHUR: What has happened to your hair?

OSCAR: It's gone quite gold!

OCTAVIA: (*As* OSCAR *helps her up*) With grief! Mister
Wilde, I must warn you I have strong reservations
about permitting my niece to marry a man with
a skeleton in his closet! As for my coiffure, it is a
shambles—and I have no idea why.

OSCAR: You have no memory of last night?

OCTAVIA: Only that I slept quite badly. Florence and I
shall return to London at once. (*She looks behind them.*)
Florence!

(FLORENCE *has risen through the clearing haze, looking*
somewhat dazed but healthy. There are no marks on her
neck. OCTAVIA *goes to her without hesitation, but the men*
hold back.)

OSCAR & BRAM: (*Both going toward her*) Florence!

(*They stop and look at each other a moment.*)

OSCAR: (*Delighted but cautious*) You're...well.

FLORENCE: (*Dazed*) I feel as though something horrid
has been burned out of me from within.

OSCAR: (*Taking her in his arms*) It has, dearest, been
burned out of all our lives.

(FLORENCE *suddenly looks into* OSCAR'*s eyes, gasps, then*
struggles to get away as he holds her.)

OSCAR: What is it, Florence?

FLORENCE: (*Forcing herself to look into his eyes*) You... have killed me, Oscar.

OSCAR: But you live! And I love you!

FLORENCE: (*Quietly*) I know. But I am too afraid. Forgive me.

OSCAR: Can you not trust me?

FLORENCE: No! Now that I've seen you through his eyes. (*Crying, she breaks from him and starts to run from the room.*)

OSCAR: Florence!

BRAM: (*Stepping in her way*) Florence.

FLORENCE: (*Looking in his eyes*) Oh, Bram, please just take me away.

(BRAM *looks at* OSCAR.)

OCTAVIA: That has been my dearest wish since rising this morning. (*Takes* FLORENCE's *arm and leads her out*) Why I was sleeping under a table in the hallway I shall never know.

(FLORENCE *and* OCTAVIA *are gone.*)

(ARTHUR *and* BRAM *just look at* OSCAR, *who is devastated.*)

BRAM: Wilde, I—

ARTHUR: Oh, do shut up, Stoker.

OSCAR: (*Smiles bravely*) I saved her. The memory at least is precious.

ARTHUR: I'd rather we didn't remember it.

BRAM: What?

ARTHUR: One word of this in London and we'll all be branded mad. We'd none of us have a career after consorting with vampires. It completely lacks reason.

OSCAR: Reason be damned—we saw it! I drank his blood.

(*They stare.*)

OSCAR: I've made love to death.

ARTHUR: Gentlemen, I'm asking you to swear silence.

OSCAR: Creatures such as Dvapara breed in secrecy and darkness.

BRAM: (*Examining the wardrobe*) Why look at this!

ARTHUR: (*Pricking his thumb with his syringe*) A blood swear, gentlemen.

BRAM: His cape isn't even singed.

OSCAR: We're changed, transubstantiated!

ARTHUR: Burn it.

BRAM: (*Putting on the cape*) No, I've quite admired it from the first.

OSCAR: We have witnessed the devil make manifest the power of God!

BRAM: (*Pricking his thumb with the syringe*) Arthur is right. We have our reputations to think of.

OSCAR: Reputations be damned—!

BRAM: And Miss Balcombe's.

OSCAR: (*Looks at them, sighs heavily*) Ah. Florence. Then let us deny the miracle thrice before cockcrow. But must it be a blood swear? Can't we simply trust each other?

(*They just look at him.*)

OSCAR: In saving our lives, we lose our innocence. (*Pricking his thumb with the syringe.*) By the pricking of my thumbs—

ALL THREE: Something wicked this way comes.

ARTHUR: Plagiarist.

BRAM: Really, Wilde, if you plan to become a professor of aesthetics, you must learn to be more obscure.

ARTHUR: (*As they jam their thumbs together*) We swear never to speak—

BRAM: (*Looking at* OSCAR) —Nor write—

ARTHUR: —About this evening ever again in our lives. I, Arthur Conan Doyle, so swear.

BRAM: I, Abraham Stoker, so swear.

OSCAR: I, Oscar Fingall O'Flahertie Wills Wilde, so swear.

(*They shudder as blood mingles, then suck their thumbs.*)

BRAM: (*Dashing out with a flourish of the cape*) Gentlemen, I must see to Florence. Good morning.

ARTHUR: I've some details to attend to as well, Oscar, before I return to Edinburgh.

OSCAR: Tell me, Arthur. Dvapara's tribe—the Nagas—

ARTHUR: Headhunters nowadays. They practice a very primitive religion.

OSCAR: But in prehistory—?

ARTHUR: They were...sun worshippers.

OSCAR: Ah. Science is certainly a colder comfort.

ARTHUR: (*Looking at the syringe as he replaces it in his bag*) We each take comfort where we may. Farewell, Oscar. (*He leaves.*)

OSCAR: Sun worshippers. (*Calling after him*) An important piece of evidence to have overlooked, my friend. I hope you've no plans to take up amateur detective work.

(*As* OSCAR *strokes the linga gently, almost as if hypnotized,* MISS QUIMBY *rises out of her coffin, looking puzzled. She feels her neck, then wanders out of the room through the hall*

door. OSCAR *does not see her. After a moment,* OCTAVIA
appears in the doorway with a very serious look on her face.
Having wiped away the blood, she looks almost pretty with
her new golden hair. She watches OSCAR *stroke the linga,*
then she snatches up one of DVAPARA'*s bones.* OSCAR *sees*
her.)

OSCAR: Fire-cracked bones—the secrets of the ages,
dear lady.

OCTAVIA: (*Clutching the bone, smiling*) And portents of
the future.

FLORENCE: (*Offstage*) Aunt, do hurry!

OCTAVIA: (*Formally*) Good day, Mister Wilde.

(OCTAVIA *leaves.* OSCAR *strokes the linga and squints into*
the brilliant dawn. TY *appears in the French door, bathed in*
morning light. He and OSCAR *stare at each other, thinking*
of the future.)

END OF PLAY